IN HER VOICE

In Her Voice

Stories of Women in the Bible

Vivia Lawton Fowler

Paulist Press
New York / Mahwah, NJ

Cover images: "One More Chapter" (foreground) by NostalgicArtHouse / Shutter stock.com; "Vector" (background) by Xennya / Depositphotos.com
Cover and book design by Lynn Else

Library of Congress Cataloging-in-Publication Data
Names: Fowler, Vivia Lawton, author.
Title: In her voice: stories of women in the Bible / Vivia Lawton Fowler.
Description: Paperback. | New York: Paulist Press, [2025] | Summary: "The stories in this collection recount the lives of twenty-five women in the Bible from a first-person perspective to bring to life the women and deepen readers' understanding of their lives"—Provided by publisher.
Identifiers: LCCN 2024051567 (print) | LCCN 2024051568 (ebook) | ISBN 9780809157433 (paperback) | ISBN 9780809189113 (ebook)
Subjects: LCSH: Women in the Bible. | Bible stories, English.
Classification: LCC BS575 .F69 2025 (print) | LCC BS575 (ebook) | DDC 220.8/3054—dc23/eng/20250215
LC record available at https://lccn.loc.gov/2024051567
LC ebook record available at https://lccn.loc.gov/2024051568

ISBN 978-0-8091-5743-3 (paperback)
ISBN 978-0-8091-8911-3 (ebook)

Published by Paulist Press
997 Macarthur Boulevard
Mahwah, NJ 07430
www.paulistpress.com

Printed and bound in the
United States of America

To my husband, Richard,
and all others who have encouraged me and
helped to shape these stories

Contents

Preface.....ix

Acknowledgments.....xi

Chapter 1. Hagar.....1

Chapter 2. The Daughters of Lot.....6

Chapter 3. Leah.....12

Chapter 4. Tamar.....17

Chapter 5. Miriam.....22

Chapter 6. The Nameless Woman.....28

Chapter 7. Deborah and Jael.....33

Chapter 8. Jephthah's Daughter.....40

Chapter 9. Hannah.....44

Chapter 10. Michal.....49

Chapter 11. Abigail.....55

Chapter 12. Bathsheba.....62

Chapter 13. Tamar, Daughter of David.....68

Chapter 14. Jezebel.....74

Chapter 15. Huldah.....79

Chapter 16. Esther.....85

Chapter 17. The Innkeeper.....91

Chapter 18. The Shepherd..96
Chapter 19. Mary, Mother of Jesus..100
Chapter 20. Jairus's Wife..107
Chapter 21. The Samaritan Woman..112
Chapter 22. The Woman Caught in Adultery..........................118
Chapter 23. Mary Magdalene..123
Chapter 24. Phoebe..128

Preface

In Her Voice: Stories of Women in the Bible is a collection of stories that invite the reader to hear the voices of biblical women and to imagine having a conversation with the woman. Each story begins with a critical point in the life of the woman, working backward to explain how she came to that point. Originally written as monologues to be performed "in character," the stories are versatile enough to use for individual or group Bible study, for study of the role of women in biblical times, for presentation to groups, and in some cases, for worship. They can be read aloud, followed by a facilitated discussion, or presented dramatically in the Chautauqua style of character presentation by one who has studied the biblical and cultural context, in order to offer pre- and post-presentation commentary and tell the character's story with such intimacy as to answer audience questions from the first-person perspective with accuracy and authenticity.

This style of biblical character presentation is a memorable and effective method of engaging participants in a conversation about the theology, history, and culture of the Bible, especially as they pertain to women. For a session of approximately one hour, the presenter should begin with a brief background on the biblical context, then signal that the teacher is going to become the character. Remind the audience that there will be a time to ask questions of the character, but she can only answer what she knows. I just use a simple shawl to signal that I am going "into character," and at the end of the monologue I say, "Do you have any questions for me?"

There usually comes a point in the Q & A session when someone asks a question that the character can't answer, such as, "When did you die?" That's a good time to remove the shawl and say, "Okay, let's talk about that." The presenter can then debrief and clarify which parts of the story were biblical and which were fictional.

Some of these stories beg to be combined into a short series, such as "Women in Genesis," or "King David's Women," or "Women Who Followed Jesus." The two short nativity stories, "The Innkeeper" and "The Shepherd," were written for Christmas Eve services and designed to be family friendly. The presenter may even wish to use props such as a stuffed sheep or a sheepdog puppet. In other stories, the presenter may embellish the narrative with asides or comments directed to the audience.

In this approach to biblical storytelling, the women are not glamorized or idealized. Their stories are tragic and hopeful, often troubling and occasionally humorous, but always instructional and inspirational. Many of the stories contain sexually explicit references, because the biblical narrative involves sexually explicit content. The stories describe women who were blessed, bartered, betrothed, and butchered; women who were mothers and martyrs; women who were warriors and murderers. They tell stories of women who questioned God, who raged against God, and who loved God. Some of the stories sound like they were plucked from current headlines, but they are thousands of years old. They are timeless, and they deserve to be told.

A note about biblical quotations: Direct quotations from the biblical text are followed by a citation (book, chapter, verse). Other quotations without a citation are fictional dialogue.

Acknowledgments

I have been writing and telling these stories over a period of more than two decades for the classroom, for special presentations to groups, and for worship and Bible study, so there are many people to acknowledge for their encouragement, assistance, and helpful feedback.

First, I want to thank the thousands of students I have taught over the years in Columbia College and Wesleyan College religious studies classes whose insightful, often troubled, questions led me to imagine how these biblical women might answer their questions. I would also like to acknowledge the Wesleyan Academy for Lifelong Learning, a group of senior adults who cannot seem to get enough of Women in the Bible presentations. I have offered a four-week series to that inquisitive group every year for more than ten years—in person and virtually. They ask great questions to the character herself, and when she answers, I always learn something.

Many thanks, also, to all the staff at Paulist Press: Paul McMahon, publisher; Leah Arabia, production editor; and especially Mary Dern Walker, in-house editor, for her careful editing of the original manuscript and for shepherding me through the editorial process. She helped translate scripts designed for stand-alone oral presentations into a book of women's stories that flows from the Old Testament to the New Testament.

I am most grateful to my husband, Richard, who was often the first to hear each story. He is the one who encouraged me to publish them so that others would be able to listen to the voices of women in the Bible.

1
Hagar

Genesis 12:10–12; 16; 21; 25; 28:6–9

I never quite understood what events preceded our departure from Egypt. I was a gift to the foreigner Abram from my master, Pharaoh. Abram had given Sarai, his sister, to Pharaoh in exchange for a great wealth of property—including me, Hagar.

But then strange things began to happen. Everyone in Pharaoh's court became ill with fever, and his wives and children developed boils all over their skin. Pharaoh's wise men and sorcerers suggested that the new woman, Sarai, was the cause of the plague, and when my master confronted Abram, Abram admitted that Sarai was not only his sister but also his wife. How is that possible, I wondered, and could that be the cause of the plague? We left in haste: Abram, Sarai, their nephew Lot, his family, and me, along with other slaves. We headed toward Canaan and settled in the Negeb.

I adored Sarai. How my heart ached to see how her barrenness overwhelmed her with sadness. I heard her tell Abram one night, "You see that the Lord has prevented me from bearing children; go in to my slave-girl; it may be that I shall obtain children by her" (Gen 16:2). Soon afterward, Abram called to me one night to come to his tent. He took me to himself, as husbands do to their wives. Sarai couldn't wait for the new moon to come, and when it did (and when the way of women did not come upon me), we were both overjoyed.

At first, Abram and Sarai pampered me as if I were a queen. But one of the other slaves told me I should not speak of *my* child, because the child was Sarai's. I thought I could do it, give up the child I bore, but as it grew within me, I became attached to the baby.

Sarai noticed my pride and happiness, and one night I heard her tell Abram, "May the wrong done to me be on you! I gave my slave-girl to your embrace, and when she saw that she had conceived, she looked on me with contempt. May the Lord judge between you and me!" (Gen 16:5). The next morning Sarai called me to her tent and showed me a side of her I had not known. How could she have such hatred for me? I feared for my life and the life of the child I carried within me. And so, I ran away, with no food, no water, no direction.

I wandered into the wilderness between Kadesh and Bered, not knowing where I would go or how I would eat. I was so thirsty by the end of the day that I fell, exhausted, in the hot sand. I thought I heard a voice say, "Hagar, slave-girl of Sarai, where have you come from and where are you going?" (Gen 16:8). I opened my eyes, thinking I was dreaming...or dying. Suddenly, I heard the voice again, saying:

> Return to your mistress, and submit to her....I will so greatly multiply your offspring that they cannot be counted for multitude....Now you have conceived and shall bear a son; you shall call him Ishmael, for the Lord has given heed to your affliction. He shall be a wild ass of a man, with his hand against everyone, and everyone's hand against him; and he shall live at odds with all his kin. (Gen 16:9–12)

Whose voice was I hearing, and what did these words mean? I could only imagine that it was an angel of the Lord, or perhaps even the Lord God, the God of whom Abram and Sarai so often spoke. They called God Yahweh; I called God El-roi—the God who sees. I wondered, "Have I really seen God and remained alive after seeing him?" (Gen 16:13). I returned to Abram and Sarai, but I wondered what kind of life lay ahead for my son and me.

Finally, the baby arrived, and I named my boy Ishmael. It means "God hears." You see, God heard two prayers: mine and Sarai's. Sarai was seventy-six and Abram was eighty-six when Ishmael was born; they had waited many years for this blessing, and I was pleased to share the blessing with them.

But hard as I tried, I could not contain my pride and joy. I didn't mean to offend Sarai, but I just couldn't hold back my pleasure at being a mother. Can you imagine bearing a precious child and giving it over to another to claim as her own? Why shouldn't I be honored as a wife of Abram? I was the one who gave him a son. The other slaves heard Sarai say I was becoming too haughty; they tried to warn me.

One night—I had not seen my son for two whole days because she had taken him to another nursemaid—I went to Sarai in anger and demanded she return my son to me. What was I thinking, talking to my mistress like that? She reminded me that I was her slave, and because she owned me, she owned whatever I produced, including my son, Ishmael. She told me that if I ever again forgot my place in her family, she would send me back to Egypt.

I silenced my anger, buried my will, and loved my boy. Thirteen years later, a miracle happened. When Sarai was eighty-nine, her handmaids began to say that she was with child. She rarely left her tent, and many of us thought she was ill, but when she was ninety, she bore a son and called him Isaac. What an appropriate name; it means, "he laughs." Nobody believed it was possible—even Sarai, who had begun to call herself Sarah. She had laughed for nine months, and Abram, who now called himself Abraham, was amazed that he would become a father at the age of one hundred. They told everyone it was the fulfillment of God's promise—their new names and their new son.

Finally, I thought, Ishmael would be mine, alone. But I didn't expect to be forgotten. Soon it became apparent that I meant nothing to them, and I heard that Sarah even feared that I might one day claim my son's place as Abraham's firstborn. Truly, I was happy for Sarah, but I did expect to receive the same support from Abraham and Sarah that I had always had. Alas, it would not be so.

I think Isaac's weaning ceremony dealt the final blow. Isaac was three, and Ishmael, my son, was about seventeen. We were celebrating the passage of our master's son from infant to young child, when Ishmael, who loved his brother, Isaac, held him up in his arms and swung him around, presenting him with pride to the family. What did Sarah see in that brotherly affection that threatened her? Her anger was evident. She insisted that Abraham send me away immediately. What would I do?

Once again, I was thrust into the desert with my son, now a young man, with only some bread and a skin of water to sustain us. We wandered in the wilderness near Beersheba for days. When the bread and water were no more, I sent my son to rest under a bush, knowing he would soon die. I couldn't bear to watch. But once again, I heard the voice of an angel of the Lord say, "Do not be afraid; for God has heard the voice of the boy where he is. Come lift up the boy and hold him fast with your hand, for I will make a great nation of him" (Gen 21:17–18).

I opened my eyes, raised my weak head, and saw a well of water before me. We drank, my boy and me, and soon gained enough strength to journey to the land of Paran.

You may wonder what became of us. We settled in Paran. I found a wife for my son from among my people, the Egyptians. My son grew strong and prospered. He had twelve sons, who became princes, the twelve princes of Arabia. God's promise was fulfilled: Ishmael's offspring became a great nation.

I learned, many years later, that Isaac, son of Sarah and Abraham, had a son named Jacob who also had twelve sons. They became the twelve tribes of Israel. My son, Ishmael, has had a hard time forgiving the family of Abraham for rejecting him. Oh, he finally received gifts—he, along with the sons of Abraham by other concubines—but Isaac was called the firstborn. It was as if Ishmael had never existed. Isaac received the name, the inheritance, everything.

Do you know Esau? Esau is the brother of Jacob, the son of Isaac, the grandson of Abraham. Esau, too, lost the inheritance of the firstborn. One of his servants arrived today. He said that Esau wanted a wife, and he wanted one of Ishmael's daughters. I am an old woman, but I think I know what is happening. It never ends—the revenge—and we women suffer the most. Does Esau want to punish his own parents, Isaac and Rebekah, by marrying the daughter of his father's archrival, Ishmael? What will become of my granddaughter,

Basemath, when she becomes Esau's third wife? Will he love her? She is so sweet, so beautiful, so innocent.

What will become of my people, the Egyptians, and my son's people, the Arabs? What will become of Abraham and Sarah's people, the Israelites? Every morning and every evening I go to the well to draw water. I listen for the voice of El-roi, but I do not hear the voice. Speak to me, El-roi. I am the one who saw God and lived. I am Hagar. Please do not forget me.

2
The Daughters of Lot

Genesis 11—19

How do you define "family?" Must it be those who are related to you by blood or marriage? Are there some you call "cousin" who are not really your cousins? Do you have blood relatives you would rather not call family? My sister and I are raising our sons together, with no man to call husband or father. But our father, Lot, is father to us and to our sons. How can that be, you ask? Let me tell you my story.

I am the younger daughter of Lot. My sister and I were born in the land of Sodom, many years after my father migrated to the land of Canaan with his uncle, Abram, who is now called Abraham. He was the son of Abraham's brother, Haran, and as the son of one of his father's very young wives, Lot was much younger than Abraham. Abraham and my father went south, finally settling in the Negeb. Both families were rich and powerful and had flocks so large that Abraham suggested they separate and settle in different lands. He allowed my father to choose first, and my father chose well. He would often describe the land with longing in his eyes, saying, "The plain of the Jordan was well watered everywhere like the garden of the LORD, like the land of Egypt, in the direction of Zoar" (Gen

13:10). He loved that land, especially the town he chose for his home: Sodom. Abraham settled in Hebron.

Father told stories that frightened me, like the time the kings of the five great Cities of the Plain—Zeboim, Admah, Gomorrah, Sodom, and Zoar—went to battle with the kings of Elam, Goiim, Shinar, and Ellasar. As the kings of Sodom and Gomorrah fled, they fell into the bitumen pits that were all over the land. Do you know about bitumen? It is a slimy tar that we use to coat our boats or bind our bricks together. The pits are all around the Salt Sea. As children, we were warned not to go near the bitumen pits. We could get stuck in the gooey tar, and if a spark of fire came near them, they could burst into flames! Oh, but back to the story. With the kings dead, the victors raided the cities of Sodom and Gomorrah and took everything, including our father, Lot! His brave uncle, Abraham, amassed an army from his large family and rescued our father and the others captured from Sodom.

My father told me stories about how the people of Sodom never recovered from that injustice, and how their bitterness made them angry, mean, and inhospitable. We were the only ones in Sodom who worshipped the Lord God. The others worshiped the gods of the Canaanites. Nevertheless, our father remained there.

My life is separated into two parts: before the firestorm and after. Father came home one night with two strangers. My mother said they were angels sent by God. Our father believed in the ancient laws of hospitality—unlike our neighbors in Sodom—and he insisted that the strangers come to our home to feast and to rest overnight. Such was our culture, to offer hospitality to the stranger, and to protect the stranger for the three days following.

"But before they lay down, the men of the city, the men of Sodom, both young and old, all the people to the last man, surrounded the house; and they called to [our father], 'Where are the men who came to you tonight? Bring them out to us, so that we may know them'" (Gen 19:4–5).

How hateful can one be? When angry people come together in their collective anger, horrible things can happen. But why would they want to molest our guests so profanely? My sister and I hid in the house with our mother and the guests, not knowing what might happen with such an angry mob. Still, we could never have guessed our father's response: "I beg you, my brothers, do not act so wickedly. Look, I have two daughters who have not known a man; let me bring them out to you, and do to them as you please; only do nothing to these men, for they have come under the shelter of my roof" (Gen 19:7–8).

My sister and I gasped, and our mother pulled us to her, covering our mouths with her hands so the angry mob would not hear us shriek in horror. How could a father sacrifice the virginity of his two daughters—perhaps even their lives—to protect strangers?

One of the men shouted threats to our father: "This fellow came here as an alien, and he would play the judge! Now we will deal worse with you than with them" (Gen 19:9). The whole mob pushed against the door, but our guests, the strangers who had come under the protection of our father, pulled him into the house and shut the door. My mother extinguished all the lamps in the house. It was so dark outside the men couldn't find the doors or windows. They groped around like blind men, and finally, miraculously, they went away.

We were terrified. We asked the strangers what we should do. They said, "Have you anyone else here? Sons-in-law, sons, daughters, or anyone you have in the city—bring them out of the place. For we are about to destroy this place, because the outcry against its people has become great before the LORD, and the LORD has sent us to destroy it" (Gen 19:12–14).

Who were these men? How could they destroy our city? Why would they save us?

We were young, my sister and I. Too young to marry, but we had been betrothed. Our father went to our husbands-to-be and urged them to leave Sodom with us. They refused. The next morning, the strangers urged us to leave, but my father lingered. He didn't want to leave his home. He was a rich man with many possessions.

And then the rumblings began. At first the ground fluttered, then the jars of water in the courtyard shook so hard they broke. It was an earthquake.

The strangers seized us by the hand and led us outside the city and said, "Flee for your life; do not look back or stop anywhere in the Plain; flee to the hills, or else you will be consumed" (Gen 19:17). But my father begged, "Oh, no, my lords; your servant has found favor with you, and you have shown me great kindness in saving my life; but I cannot flee to the hills, for fear the disaster will overtake me and I die. Look, that city is near enough to flee to, and it is a little one. Let me escape there—is it not a little one?—and my life will be saved!" (Gen 19:18–20).

As we looked around the Cities of the Plains, we saw the earth explode with fire, and the salty sea churn as if it were being stirred by the gods. Huge chunks of salt were thrown up and cast out of the sea, impaling the ground where they landed. Those pillars of salt looked like a multitude of ashen refugees, fleeing from the firestorm. Who were these strangers who could cause such a disaster? Was this the work of the Lord God, about whom my father had spoken?

Finally, one of the visitors said, "Very well, I grant you this favor too, and will not overthrow the city of which you have spoken. Hurry, escape there, for I can do nothing until you arrive there" (Gen 19:21–22). We ran as hard as we could. We dropped everything we were carrying, eager to save our lives. My sister and I were young and agile, and at some point, we were separated from our parents. When we neared the town of Zoar, we stopped, exhausted from our escape.

Over the horizon we saw our father's shape emerge, but he was alone. "Where is your mother?" he asked. "I thought she was with you." But she was not with us, and she did not appear in the minutes that followed. We never saw her again.

Our father was never the same after that. We settled in a cave in the hills of Zoar. We never explored our surroundings, certain we were the only people there. Our father believed that the Lord God had destroyed all humans, including our mother. He kept saying, "It was her fault. She should never have looked back. They told us not to look back." I never thought it was her fault. She didn't do anything wrong.

Day after day, father would gaze down on the plains covered with ash and look upon the multitude of ash-covered pillars of salt that had been thrust from the Sea of Salt. He would ask, "Is that your mother? Perhaps that one?" He would cry at night: "Who will carry on my name? I have no wife. My daughters have no sons." I feared he was going mad. He began to drink strong wine every night until he was drunk enough to fall into a fitful sleep.

Not long after we settled in the caves near Zoar, my sister began to bleed between her legs. Our mother told us that would happen; we missed her so much. Our father told her she was a woman now, and if we were back in Sodom, she would be ready to marry. Soon after, it happened to me, too.

One night, our father, in one of his drunken stupors, fell onto my sister as she was sleeping and began to thrust himself into her. He covered her mouth so she would not scream out in pain and horror, but I knew what was happening. Our mother had told us about that, too, but she didn't tell us that fathers did it to their daughters. Then he came to me. My own father. I never thought I could be more disappointed in him than the day he offered us to the men of Sodom in exchange for protection of our visitors, but now I know an even greater disappointment. I don't hate him, but my heart is broken. My own father. He said it was our duty to give him sons.

Soon we were both pregnant, my sister and I. That's another thing our mother told us about. And soon we learned we were not the only ones to survive the firestorm. We encountered others, and they asked where our husbands were. Father could have made up a story about their untimely death, but instead he blamed us for our predicament. He told them he heard us conspiring one night, saying:

> "Come, let us make our father drink wine, and we will lie with him, so that we may preserve offspring through our father." So, they made [me] drink wine that night; and the firstborn went in, and lay with [me]; [I pretended I] did not know when she lay down or when she rose. On the next day, the firstborn said to the younger, "Look I lay last night with my father; let us make him drink wine tonight also; then you go in and lie with him, so that we may preserve offspring through our father." So they made [me] drink wine that night also; and the younger rose, and lay

> with [me]; and [I pretended I] did not know when she lay down or when she rose. (Gen 19:32–35)

That was his story. Today I tell you the true story. Why did I keep this secret for so long? I was ashamed, and hurt, and after all, who would believe my story over my father's?

When my sister bore her son, she named him Moab. When I bore a son, I named him Ben-Ammi. Our father gloated: "My family will become a great nation, just like the nation promised to my uncle, Abraham."

It has been many years, and our father has died. We have grown old, and our sons have married and had sons and daughters of their own. Their people, the Moabites and the Ammonites, have become strong. But it seems that there is never enough land or possessions or slaves to satisfy everyone. Perhaps it was not only the Sodomites who were greedy and selfish.

I pray to the Lord God of my father that our sons and grandsons will welcome strangers and seek peace and that our people will establish laws that protect their daughters and granddaughters—laws that will protect their bodies from men who wish to abuse them, even their own fathers.

3
Leah

Genesis 28—35

I know what you must think about me: "She's the one who took her sister's husband from her. How could she do that?" But you don't really know me, and you don't really understand how it is in my family—or for that matter, for most women I know. And now my own daughter has discovered the way of women and men. How I wish I could have protected her.

My name is Leah. My father is Laban of Haran. We come from a large family—the family of Terah. You probably don't know my great-grandfather, Nahor, but you may know his brother and sister, Abraham and Sarah. I think my grandfather Bethuel was always jealous of his uncle Abraham. Abraham: the wealthy one. Abraham: the powerful one. Abraham: the favored one. But he wasn't so jealous that he objected to arranging the marriage of his daughter, Rebekah, to Abraham's son, Isaac.

You might wonder why we marry such close relations. The reasons are simple: to keep our family pure, to strengthen the clan's property and power, and to make sure we pass to the next generation the strongest qualities. As for the women, we simply marry whomever our fathers—or brothers, if our fathers are dead—tell us to marry. We have no choice; we have no voice in the decision.

Most of the time, that is. Let me tell you about my own marriage to my husband, Jacob. He, too, is a member of our family. He is my cousin, the son of my aunt, Rebekah. In fact, he was her favorite son. His older twin brother, Esau, was his father's favorite, but he wasn't very clever. Jacob tricked him out of his birthright for the meager price of a bowl of porridge. Oh, but Esau was furious—so angry that Rebekah sent Jacob to my father's land to escape Esau's wrath, and also so he would not marry a foreign woman, as Esau had done. Esau angered his parents by marrying not one, but three foreign women: two Canaanite women and one Arabian woman—a daughter of Ishmael, his father Isaac's half-brother and archrival. Jacob's family criticized Esau for his actions, but I have always sympathized with him. I know how it feels not to be the favored one.

Jacob should have come for me. I was the elder sister, but the first woman of Haran Jacob saw after his long journey was my younger sister, Rachel. Can you blame him for loving her at first sight? "Sweet Rachel," my father says, "like a little ewe lamb." And me—Father loves me, too. He tells me I'm as strong as a cow and with eyes to match. Upon meeting Rachel, Jacob was elated to see one of his relatives and relieved to know that he would soon experience hospitality at the tent of my father.

The first thing he did was ask for Rachel to be his wife. Why Rachel? She was not even old enough to marry. I was, but he didn't ask for me. He loved Rachel so much that he was willing to wait seven years for her, seven years of service to my father in exchange for the bride price he did not have, because he was estranged from his family.

Jacob underestimated my father, and he underestimated me. My father is a deceitful man who will do anything to profit himself. And he wants so badly to be rich and powerful. Perhaps he got that from his own father and his father before him. Perhaps I, too, have inherited evil qualities from him. Nothing made my father happier than to think that the grandson of Abraham should be beholden to him and that he might profit from Jacob's hard work. And he did profit.

I confess that I used my father's obsession to my advantage. "Father," I said, as the men prepared for the marriage celebration, "Are you going to give away your precious daughter Rachel for a mere seven years' work? Why don't you dress me in the wedding veil and take me into the tent? That way you can rid yourself of two daughters at the same time. Once Jacob discovers that I am his wife, he will probably work another seven years for Rachel. You know how much he loves her. You can tell him that it is our custom that the older sister must be wed first."

You see, I had to do it. There are not many men in Haran of our family's status for us to marry. And I was getting old. Who would want me? Men don't want strong women. They want sweet, gentle women like Rachel. It was easy, too. The men celebrated in the tent of our father, Laban, for days, while the women prepared Rachel in their tent.

Late one night, Laban sent word to the women's tent that the men's celebration would be extended another day. That was my signal; time for our deception to begin. I left the tent, feigning sickness, and wrapped myself in Rachel's marriage veil. I met Father outside the tent that was prepared for Jacob and his bride, and he led me into the tent in silence. Jacob entered a few minutes later, and Father closed the entrance to the tent.

Jacob stumbled over to where I lay on the pillows and fell on top of me. His breath smelled of strong wine, and he was quickly aroused. I said nothing, and for a moment, I thought he noticed that my body felt a little firmer and a little fuller than he might have expected Rachel's to feel, but it was dark, and he had waited seven years for that night.

It wasn't until morning that he realized he had, in fact, taken me for his wife. Maybe he knew and didn't care. One wife...two... four...more sons...more wealth...more power—what difference does it make? But Rachel was furious when she discovered the deception. I told her it really didn't matter if we shared this man or the next one that might come along; such is common in our tradition. Jacob appeared angry, too, but Father told him he could have my maidservant, Zilpah, as a concubine, and at the end of the week of celebration, he could have Rachel and her maidservant, Bilhah—as long as he worked seven more years for our father. That satisfied him.

I thought I would be happy, but I was not. Neither was Rachel. I did not have the love of my husband, and Rachel could not give him a son. I gave him eight sons altogether: six by myself and two from my maidservant Zilpah. Rachel's maidservant, Bilhah, gave him two sons before Rachel finally bore Joseph. And then Rachel died giving birth to Benjamin.

Strangely enough, we sisters found solace in each other. And we found solace in prayer. We prayed to el-Shaddai, the god of the mountain and to Elohim, the high god. I prayed for love; Rachel prayed for sons. I suppose our prayers were answered, but not in the way we expected. Rachel finally got her sons, and I got love. Not the love I wanted from my husband, but an indescribable love from God.

After giving birth to Benjamin—it was a very difficult birth—Rachel breathed her final breaths while I held her in my arms. I told her that I did not believe God had closed her womb and opened mine—like our tradition said. And I asked for her forgiveness for deceiving her. She smiled at me and kissed my hand and called me "beloved." I cried for days after she died. Rachel—the sweet, gentle, frail one—had the strength to forgive.

Forgiveness is cathartic, is it not? Jacob tells me he knows how I feel—being forgiven, that is. You see, he and his brother, Esau, reconciled as we journeyed on our way back to Bethel after finally leaving my father's home. We had to pass through Esau's territory, Edom, and word came to us that Esau and four hundred men were coming in our direction. We assumed they meant harm, so Jacob lined us up in order of reverse priority, to protect the favored ones from harm: Rachel's sons last, and then my sons, and so on. But they did not attack; instead, Esau greeted his estranged brother with a kiss of welcome (Gen 33). That was memorable for all of us: a family reunited. I want to be able to forgive like that, but I cannot seem to bring myself to forgive and forget what happened to my daughter, Dinah.

Sweet Dinah. She is lovely, like her aunt, Rachel. Shechem, a young prince, loved her at first sight—just like Jacob did when he saw Rachel. She loved him too, she told me, even though he was not one of us. He knew he was wrong to take her by force; he knew he had violated her, but he begged his father to make amends with her father so that she could be his wife.

I was furious that a man would rape my precious daughter. Jacob was furious because he was an uncircumcised man, but he did not want to make enemies. Our sons did not have as much restraint as their father, but they certainly inherited the tendency to deceive that runs in my family.

Shechem and his father said that they would do anything to reconcile with our family, so my sons Simeon and Levi suggested that they agree to be circumcised—all the men of Shechem—and then their men could marry our daughters and our men could marry their daughters. They agreed! And while they were healing, Simeon and Levi went into their town, killed all the men, and plundered the wealth of the city. They brought poor, grief-stricken Dinah home to me, and for months I feared she would take her own life—or die of grief.

She vows she will never forgive her brothers for killing her husband, and she cannot forgive her own father for not stopping them. They defended themselves, saying, "Should our sister be treated like a whore?" (Gen 34:31). But the truth is, they only wanted to be powerful. To Jacob, it only mattered that he might lose his good name. Dinah's wishes did not matter. Power and property—it always comes down to that.

When will this end? When will the men we love, whose sons we bear, whose gods we revere—when will they cease using us for their gain? Abraham passed his wife off as his sister so that he would not be killed, not once but twice. Isaac did the same with Rebekah and King Abimelech. Jacob abandoned his own daughter to save his reputation. And they all profited along the way—at our expense. I hate this resentment that I feel! Please, God, help me find the strength of my sister, Rachel, to forgive. Please, God, give my precious Dinah peace of mind. Please, God, heal the evil that we pass from generation to generation—the evil that proclaims women are the property of men, barrenness is a curse from God, and daughters are less important than sons. Deliver us from this evil, O God. In your blessed name, I pray. Amen.

4
Tamar

Genesis 38

Twins! Do you know anyone who has raised twins? How do mothers manage? My boys always seem to be at odds with each other. They started fighting when they shared my womb, and they fought over who would be the first one out! Even today, they fight over who will receive the inheritance of the firstborn son.

I am a Canaanite, born and raised in the town of Timnah. As a young girl, I was betrothed to a man named Er, from the family of Judah. I had heard stories about Judah, his father Jacob, his grandfather Isaac, and his great-grandfather Abraham. They were a large, wealthy, and powerful family. I always wondered why Judah left his family. Some of the slaves he brought with him said that he feared that his older brother, Reuben, would kill him for selling his younger brother, Joseph, to a caravan of Ishmaelites, traveling to Egypt. Others said he was so ashamed of himself for selling his brother into slavery that he could not bear to continue living with his family.

I found it odd that this man, Judah, married a Canaanite woman and found another Canaanite woman for his son, Er, to marry—me. Had he rejected his family? Had they rejected him? Had he rejected the God of Abraham and the traditions of his people? I never found him to be a mean man, but his son Er was. He was violent. I was afraid of him.

When the men came running in from the fields one day and said my husband had been struck by lightning, I didn't object when they said it was God's will—even though the god I believe in doesn't do such things to people, whether they are good or evil. But he was a wicked man, and if their people are right, I wouldn't be surprised if God struck him dead.

I didn't know much about the traditions of the Hebrew people, but one of them was called the "brother law"—*levirate* in their language. It says when a man dies before his wife bears a son to carry on his lineage, the second brother must take her as his wife—to bear a son for the first brother. I heard Judah say this to his second son, Onan: "Go in to your brother's wife and perform the duty of a brother-in-law to her; raise up offspring for your brother" (Gen 38:8; see also Deut 25:5–10).

Onan didn't like this one bit; neither did I. Onan didn't want me for his wife, nor did he want to give his dead brother the inheritance. He wanted it for himself, so he decided if he never "went in to me," eventually I would be called barren or die, whichever came first, and he would be able to have a child by another woman.

Onan didn't want his father to know about his plot, so every time he came into my bed, he spilled his seed on the bed or on the ground, but not in me. He may have fooled his father, but he didn't fool God.

Soon after he took me for his wife, the men came running in from the fields and said my second husband had been struck by lightning. I didn't object this time either when they said it was God's will, for he disobeyed the will of God and his family. I did object when his father began to accuse me of having a role in the deaths of my two husbands. He even called me a witch! And worse yet, he sent me away—back to my father's house—where I was to wait for the third son, Shelah, to be old enough to carry out the law of brothers.

Do you hear what I'm saying? First, my father *betrothed me* to Er for a modest bride price (some choice sheep and one excellent shepherd). Next my father-in-law Judah *gave me* to one son and then another, and then *sent me* back to my father to live as a widow until *he called me* back. I have no independence, no chance to marry whom

I wish, no chance to bear a son of my own—outside the boundaries of these men who control my fate.

As I wandered around the town of Timnah in my widow's garments, my heart stirred with jealousy for the freedom of youth whenever I saw the eyes of young women longing for their betrothed, or the independence of the prostitutes. I was even jealous of the prostitutes! At least they are free to go where they wish and sleep with whom they wish. At least they have a chance of becoming mothers.

Year after year, I would hear that Judah had come to Timnah for the sheepshearing (and a visit or two with the local prostitutes). Sometimes his son Shelah came to Timnah with him, and after several years I saw the young, handsome Shelah and knew he was a man, old enough to marry. But they never came for me. And suddenly I thought, "That's it! That's what I will do! I will wait no longer. I will take action." I made a plan, but I was patient. I waited a full year, until the next season for shearing the sheep.

When I heard that Judah was on his way, I took off my widow's garments and covered myself with a beautiful veil the color of the sky, a veil that covered most of my face. I sat by the entrance to Enaim, on the road to Timnah. When Judah and his caravan approached, I went to greet him, and in my softest voice asked, "Dear sir, how I might serve you during your visit?" I could tell he was aroused by my voice, the scent of my perfumes, and my offer, and he said, "Come, let me come in to you." He said he would like to negotiate for my services for the duration of his visit. "Oh, kind sir," I responded, "that will require quite a sum in advance," knowing he would not have that many coins with him. He told me he could pay me after the sheep shearing, and I asked,

> "What will you give me, that you may come in to me?" He answered, "I will send you a kid from the flock." And [I] said, "Only if you give me a pledge, until you send it. "He said, "What pledge shall I give you?" [I] replied, "Your signet and your cord, and the staff that is in your hand." (Gen 38:16–18)

And he did.

My plan worked. He was satisfied...and so was I. After he left, I removed my veil, replaced my widow's garments, and returned to my father's house, placing the collateral under my pallet. I never returned to the wall at the entrance to Enaim, but he did. At least he has some honorable traits. He returned after the sheepshearing and asked for the prostitute who sat by the wall, so he could pay his debt, but no one knew of any such prostitute. And so, he returned home.

Soon I knew I was with child. In fact, within a few months, when most women can still hide their growing bellies, mine was so large even my father suspected. He asked me, and I told him. He understood why I did what I did, but he feared for my safety. You see, I still belonged to the family of Judah, according to the Hebrew tradition, and in their tradition the elders could sentence to death a man and a woman caught in the act of adultery. Adultery was one man's offense against another man's property. But a woman who is not married, if caught pregnant, is also guilty.

My father tried to hide me, but soon others noticed the size of my growing belly. Someone told Judah: "Your daughter-in-law Tamar has played the whore; moreover, she is pregnant as a result of whoredom." Judah was furious, and he sent a mob of angry men to get me. He said, "Bring her out, and let her be burned" (Gen 38:24).

As they were bringing me out, I proudly removed my widow's veil, replaced it with my beautiful blue veil, and drew from my cloak Judah's signet, cord, and staff, and said, "It was the owner of these who made me pregnant. Take note, please, whose these are, the signet and the cord and the staff" (Gen 38:25).

You should have seen his face. He said, "She is more in the right than I, since I did not give her to my son Shelah" (Gen 38:26). No truer words were ever spoken by this man. I may have tricked him into becoming a father, but he tried to trick me out of being a mother. He took me to his home, but he never lay with me again.

As my belly grew and grew, I knew there were two babies in my womb. They were constantly at odds with each other, squirming, kicking, as if they were battling to see who would be born first.

"When the time of [my] delivery came, in the height of labor, one put out a hand; and the midwife took and bound on his hand a crimson thread, saying, 'This one came out first.' But just then he drew back his hand, and out came his brother; and she said, 'What a breach you have made for yourself!'" Therefore, he was named Perez. Afterward his brother came out with the crimson thread on his hand; and he was named Zerah (Gen 38:27–30).

I found all of this odd, but I knew how important the firstborn is in my father-in-law's tradition—or should I say the father of my sons. It's all about the promise of the covenant: God's blessing for family, land, power, prosperity. I love to remind my husband that he wasn't the first born, nor was his father, Jacob, nor was his father, Isaac. Their stories are not love stories. Many of the mothers and wives in the stories were not even loved. Many of them, like me, had to take matters into their own hands to have children, or to ensure that their favored child received the inheritance. Their stories are not faith stories. They are succession stories.

Where does faith come into these stories? I love to hear the elders talk about their God, the Creator, the one who personifies steadfast love: *hesed*. I like to think that's the meaning of covenant: God's steadfast love. Not who is first or best. Not who was chosen or the most victorious in battle. Not the richest nor the most powerful. That's what I've learned from this complicated family. Often the first is last and the last is first. Often the best leader is one who serves. Will our family ever produce men and women who live in that way? That is my prayer.

5
Miriam

Exodus 2—15; Leviticus 13:1–8; Numbers 12; 20:1; 26:59; Deuteronomy 24:8–9

I almost fear asking you this question—much less answering it myself—but have you ever wondered if God is real? Or if God listens to your prayers? Or if God even cares about what happens in your life? I must confess to you: I have wondered these things...and not just once, but several times.

My name is Miriam. For over eighty years I lived as a slave in Egypt, and for many years since, I have traveled through the wilderness of Sinai. It has taken me a long time to realize that when God seems most distant, it is because I—and not God—have wandered away from our covenant of faith.

I remember once when I was a young girl in Egypt, I wondered if God were real. You see, our family—and all the Hebrew families—were slaves of Pharaoh in Egypt. It was a horrible life. We had little to eat, and we had to work hard. Not only were we forced to build cities to store Pharaoh's grain, but we also had to make the bricks ourselves. If we failed to work hard enough, we were punished. We all worked: the old men, the pregnant women, and the small children. As a little girl, I carried jugs of water to the thirsty workers, and I would often see them being whipped by the guards. I would wipe their wounds and sing softly to them, songs about God that I composed in my quiet time alone. Singing brought me comfort. How angry I would get when I saw members of the royal family standing by smugly, watching us work. Especially Moses. You see, Moses would not admit it, but he was one of us. He may have been called a prince—adopted grandson of Pharaoh—but we knew. I knew because I was his sister.

The first time I questioned all that my mother told me about God was when Moses was born. You see, Pharaoh was so threatened by the growing number of Hebrew slaves that he decreed that all Hebrew baby boys should be killed. Had he forgotten what our ancestor, Joseph, did to save Egypt from famine? After my brother was born, Mother cried for three whole months. I do not know whether she cried out of grief or just to hide the whimpers of my baby brother. Finally, she decided to let him go—as the Egyptians sometimes did—into the hands of the gods. She put him in a basket and left him in the river to die. I remember going outside that night and shouting, "Where are you, God? Do you even care?" All I could hear was the hiss of the crocodiles as they slithered into the river.

The next day, I went down to the river to see if Moses were still there. I do not know what I would have done if I had found him dead, or drowned, or eaten by the crocodiles; nor do I know what I would have done if I had found him alive. But alas, I was not the one who found him. As I approached the river, I heard voices, and I hid in the grasses by the river's bank. It was Pharaoh's daughter; she had found the basket, and Moses was alive! When I realized she knew that it was a Hebrew baby, my heart stopped. I could hardly breathe. If she was anything like her father, she would surely kill him—maybe throw him against a rock or drown him. But she did not. Instead, she held him gently and rocked him in her arms. She talked to her maids about taking him home with her. Why would she do such a thing? Did she not have children of her own? Was he a plaything to her? Was she trying to rebel against her father, as young girls sometimes do? Or was God's hand in this? I took a deep breath and walked casually from behind the grasses and said to the princess, "Shall I go and get you a nurse from the Hebrew women to nurse the child for you?" (Exod 2:7). Can you believe she said yes? I quickly ran home and got Mother. God had answered my prayers, and she was getting another chance to raise her son. Mother was his nursemaid, but as he grew up, Moses began to ignore us.

For many years, we rarely saw him. Mother and Father died, along with many other Hebrew slaves. My brother, Aaron, and I were left alone. Again, I wondered, "God, where are you? Why do you let us suffer so?" Then one day, word came to our camp that Moses had killed an Egyptian guard who was abusing one of the Hebrew slaves. What came over him? Why would he come to our defense? We later heard he had escaped far away to the land of Midian and taken a Midianite wife. For years we heard nothing about him. And then he was back. He came to the Hebrew camp and told Aaron and me that God wanted us to take the Hebrews out of Egypt. We didn't know whether to trust him or not. Was this a trick? He seemed to be a much different person than when he left Egypt forty years ago. He told us about his encounters with God, whom he now called Yahweh. We believed him.

And can you imagine? He convinced Pharaoh to let us go! Ah, but that was the easy part. The hard part was convincing our people to leave Egypt where at least they had homes and food. "Please God," I prayed, "be with us in this time of need. Give us strength and wisdom for the days ahead." Moses and Aaron weren't having much success convincing the men to leave, so I devised a plan. I visited twelve homes—one home for each of the twelve sons of our ancestor Jacob—and talked to the women. Then I assigned each of the women to go to twelve more homes until we had met with all the Hebrew women. We prayed and fasted for three days, and then we assembled at the edge of the Hebrew camp. We brought our lamps with us, and as we stood there in the darkness of the night, the light from our lamps shone brightly, like a symbol of our courage and faith. We prayed and sang the songs of our faith, some of the songs I had taught the women to sing. Then we went to our homes and talked to the men. They agreed to go with me and with Aaron and with Moses.

That was not the only amazing thing that happened. When we reached the waters of the Sea of Reeds, we learned that Pharaoh's army was coming after us. Once again, I screamed at God, "Will you abandon us now, God? After all we have done? Do you really care about us, God?" You must be wondering by now why my faith was not stronger after all the miracles I had witnessed. I am embarrassed to admit that I said those things to God. God should have swept me away with the powerful winds that seemed to come out of nowhere. But instead, the winds pushed the waters back long enough for us to make it to land on the other side of the sea. Right after we reached dry ground, the winds subsided, the waters returned, and the Egyptian army was drowned. We were saved.

You would think that after watching the Israelites—hundreds of thousands of us—cross through the sea on dry land, and after seeing the Egyptian army drown in the swirling waters, I would never again ask if God were real. But I confess I did. You see, I began to resent Moses, and the more Moses talked about being God's prophet, the more I resented God as well. I had always thought of myself as God's prophetess, and the people trusted me. When Moses was filling his belly with fine food and strong wine, I was talking to our people about God's love. When Moses was smirking at the suffering slaves, I was bringing them water to quench their thirst. When I was organizing the women to pray and fast, Moses and Aaron were boasting of their prophecies about plagues. Moses even took credit for the song of victory that we sang for years after leaving Egypt. That was my song! I taught the people to sing:

> The Lord is my strength and my might,
> And he has become my salvation;
> This is my God, and I will praise him,
> My father's God, and I will exalt him. (Exod 15:2)

But now they call it Moses's song, not Miriam's. For years we have wandered in the wilderness of Sinai. Do you think Moses or Aaron have ever asked for my guidance? Never! And they have never asked for my suggestions about how to settle disagreements that arise in the camp either. Right now, I am angry with Moses and Aaron. And I am angry with God. A few days ago, Aaron and I were commiserating about Moses—both of us. I suppose we wanted our people to see that Moses was not the only one who had been called by God. Moses was not the only one who made sacrifices to lead the people of Israel to the Promised Land. Moses heard of our complaints and told us that God wanted to talk to the three of us. We went with him down to the tent of meeting, and there we saw the cloud that led us through the wilderness during the day. Out of the cloud came the very voice of God, and it was an angry voice. God was not pleased with Aaron and me for criticizing Moses. Our people needed strong, faithful leadership. They needed peacemakers, and we were being petty and argumentative. But I could not see that then. I could only shout in anger, "I know I offended you, God, but why do you only punish me? Why not Aaron too? He criticized Moses, just as I did. Must I have my reputation usurped by one brother and bear the punishment for another? It's not fair, God. Do you hear me, God? You're not being fair!" Right after the cloud of God lifted from the tent of meeting, my skin developed spots and soon became a grayish white all over. For seven days I sat alone outside the camp, thinking about what happened that day. The people said it was God's punishment because I criticized Moses. Moses and Aaron said so, too. That hurt. I hurt all over, even inside. For days I spoke with bitterness—not reverence—to God. Then one day I remembered that I have known many good people to have this skin affliction. In fact, I remembered one of the women I nursed some weeks ago who looked just like this and recovered. Had it transferred from her skin to mine? The healers say that happens with some diseases. I refused to blame God for what was wrong with me—even though the people said I should. The God I know and trust is a loving and just God. People get sick and die, and awful things happen, but I do not believe God punishes us like that. The rain falls on the just and the unjust, does it not? I decided that I could curse God for what was wrong with me and ask if God cared about this painful predicament I was in, or I could thank God for being as close to me at that moment as the very pulse in my veins—even though I was unclean, an outcast in the eyes of every man, woman, and child in our camp. I chose to thank God.

The next day my skin began to heal. Today it is almost clear. Tomorrow the priest will come to examine me, and if he approves, I will join my people the following day, and we can get on with our trip to the land God has promised us! I pray for forgiveness from my anger and bitterness toward God, and I pray for God to heal my bitterness toward my brothers. I pray for grace to forgive my brothers, and I pray that my brothers will respect the gifts that God has given me and allow me to use them to the glory of God and the salvation of our people. God knows that Moses cannot do this alone, not even with Aaron's help. From now on, if I ever again become so desperate, so angry, so filled with fear that I cannot even speak to God, I will remember this moment. And I will remember my songs. I will sing over and over:

> The LORD is my strength and might,
> And he has become my salvation;
> This is my God, and I will praise him,
> My father's God, and I will exalt him. (Exod 15:2)

6
The Nameless Woman

Deuteronomy 22:13–21; 24:1; Numbers 5:11–31

Note: This is not an actual character in the Bible; rather, her story reflects how the ancient laws might have affected many women like her.

My story is painful, but it is one I must tell. I'm not sure where to start. Let me begin by telling you how I came to be married.

I knew my husband for many years before we were married. As a child I watched him play with the other boys, and our families often gathered with other Israelites for festivals. Now mind you, that does not mean we knew each other well. It would not have been appropriate to talk to him in private, or to spend time with him. But I knew who he was, and I knew his family. As a child, I played games with his sister.

As I grew up, I wondered if he might be the one with whom I would spend the rest of my life. I wondered if our fathers had discussed a possible marriage. I soon discovered that they had. The marriage contract was negotiated, we were betrothed, and the bride price—some silver and a plot of land—was exchanged. It never occurred to me to wonder whether or not he would love me. I was just a child. What does a child know about these things? I had to wait until I became a woman to be his wife, and soon that day came. The blood scared me, and it was a little painful, but I was a woman! I could be married!

I was so hopeful—and nervous—the night of our wedding almost three years ago. How long I had waited for that day! I had prepared myself to be a good, pure, devoted wife—as much as I could—and my mother tried to prepare me for my wedding night—as much as she could. Would I please him? Would I give him sons? For several days I was pampered and oiled by the women while the men enjoyed food and wine and merriment. Our fathers were pleased to strengthen the alliance between our two families through marriage. It is good to have another ally when resources are scarce or when enemies threaten the security of our lands.

After the marriage ceremony, we went to the tent that had been prepared for us. I had never been this close to him, and he didn't seem to be the same cheerful young man I had observed in the village. He seemed moody, temperamental. At one moment he seemed almost angry. At another moment he looked me over with suspicion. Maybe it was the wine. Maybe it was me. And then without a word, he took me as his wife—forcefully, with no emotion and no words of love. It was not what I expected, but I'll admit it was a pleasure I'd never experienced! I tried to return the pleasure to him.

When he was finished and satisfied, his first words were to ask me if I had known another man. I was shocked by his words, and I assured him I had not. He turned away from me and quickly fell into a deep sleep. Not me! I lay awake for hours, wondering what I had done to displease my new husband.

When morning came, we awoke, and the first thing he did was throw me out of our bed and toss the bedding onto the floor of our wedding tent. And then he looked at me with a glare that spoke of mistrust and hatred. He shouted at me, but he never called me by name. He just called me woman—you unclean woman. You see, for some reason, the bedclothes showed no proof of my virginity—not even a speck of blood. But I was not unclean; I was a pure bride. I was heartbroken. And then I was frightened. His accusations, if proven true, would bring great grief to my family who promised his family a virgin. But that is only the beginning. You see, in my culture, if, after his wedding night, a man accuses his wife of not being a virgin, her father must produce proof of her virginity to the elders of the town. If there is no proof, she is stoned. And where is the proof, if there is no blood on the bedclothes?

He took me by my hair and dragged me from our wedding tent to my father's tent and accused me of adultery. Adultery! In my culture, adultery is one man's violation of another man's property, and since we were betrothed, I had been his property. I had not committed adultery, and if another man had violated me, both he and I could be accused of adultery, but I was the only one there. I was the only one accused.

I could not believe what I was hearing. This was my husband, the one who should be my beloved. Where was his love? I was devastated! But my father and mother, bless them, came to my defense. I never learned how they did it, but somehow, they produced bed sheets soiled by a spot of blood. We went before the elders and the men discussed the case. My father spoke the words of the law:

> I gave my daughter in marriage to this man but he dislikes her; now he has made up charges against her, saying, "I did not find evidence of your daughter's virginity." But here is the evidence of my daughter's virginity. (Deut 22:16–17)

Like my husband, the elders only referred to me as the woman—the unclean woman—as if I were nameless. But I was exonerated; they took my father's word over my husband's, and they fined him "one hundred shekels of silver" and ordered that he could never divorce me as long as he lives.

My husband almost looked disappointed as we went home that day. Did he want me dead? I wondered. Day after day he looked at me with that same look of mistrust. He quizzed me about where I went and what I did. He shouted at me whenever I looked at another man. I prayed for his love. I prayed for his forgiveness—even though I was unsure why I needed to be forgiven. Most of all, month after month I prayed for a son. I just knew he would love me if I gave him a son. But the blood came with the regularity of the moon.

And then one day, three months ago, I shared with him my joyful news. I was with child. Finally, the absence of blood was reason for celebration, but there was no joy on his face—only that familiar look of jealousy and mistrust. He asked me over and over if the child was his, and I assured him that it was. I hoped he would believe me. And for a while I thought he did. Then, three days ago, as we arose from sleep, there in plain view was the bloody, soiled bed sheet that I would have rejoiced to see three years ago. The pain came soon, and the nausea, and more blood. And the look on his face. Once again, he shouted at me and called me unclean. He accused me of doing something sinful to harm the unborn child. And then he dragged me before the priest who set me before the Lord Almighty. There I sat, scared, sick, in pain, and heartbroken. There I sat, in the presence of the Lord Almighty, and the priest stripped off the veil covering my head. I felt so exposed, so afraid, so alone.

The priest then carried out the ritual for the law for cases of jealousy. He scooped up some of the dust from the floor of the tabernacle and mixed it in an earthenware vessel with holy water. Holy water! Then he wrote a curse on a scroll and made me swear an oath. He said these words of the ritual:

> If no man has lain with you, if you have not turned aside to uncleanness while under your husband's authority, be immune to this water of bitterness that brings the curse. But if you have gone astray while under your husband's authority, if you have defiled yourself and some man other than your husband has had intercourse with you...the Lord make you an execration and an oath among your people, when the Lord makes your uterus drop, your womb discharge; now may this water that brings the curse enter your bowels and make your womb discharge, your uterus drop! (Num 5:19–31)

The priest told me to say, "Amen! Amen!" And I did. But he never called me by my name.

He dipped the scroll into the water, and I watched that dark ink spill into the holy water. He mixed the ink with the water and the dust from the floor and made me drink it. All of it. My head swirled; my belly ached; I was sickened by the smell of incense and burning grain from the grain offering we had brought. Scared that I would lose my child, I prayed silently to Yahweh, my God. "Is this your law, God? Do you believe me? Don't you know everything, God? Don't you know that I am pure? That I am innocent of these charges? Don't you know my name?"

Time and time again I have seen male babies circumcised on the eighth day. How often I have been reminded of the words: "So shall my covenant be in your flesh an everlasting covenant" (Gen 17:13b). I am a woman. Am I, therefore, forever to be outside of the covenant of the Lord? Why, then, am I bound by the laws of the same covenant? Or is it perhaps possible that God cares little about the circumcision of the flesh and more about purity of heart?

Somehow, I was able to walk home that day—alone, for my husband left me at the door of the tabernacle. I do not know how I managed. An old widow noticed me and came to my house to nurse me. She prepared a drink for me that eased the pain in my belly, but it did nothing to ease the pain in my heart. Three days have passed, and I have not miscarried, but neither have I spoken to my husband or him to me. If I do miscarry, I will be a pariah in my town. I will be scorned by women and men alike. Aside from my husband's punishment for his first false accusation, he would probably divorce me. Men can do that—for any reason or for no reason, but we women cannot divorce our husbands at all.

If I do not miscarry, I will be honored as a mother. How ironic. And what does the law say about my husband if I am found innocent of his accusations? It says: "The man shall be free from iniquity, but the woman shall bear her iniquity" (Num 5:31).

I pray that I have a girl child. I will raise her to be strong, to be independent, and to be faithful to God. I think I will name her Deborah.

7
Deborah and Jael

Judges 2—5; 21:25; Deuteronomy 22:23–27

It happened again. Another vision. I was meditating, seeking wisdom from God, and then it was as if I were a bird flying over a wretched scene. Usually, it was a battle. I saw the formations opposing one another, swords drawn, shields up, then the clash of the lines. Swords and shields, helmets, blood and limbs, fallen men, cries of anguish, and then silence. I heard the numbers of the dead ringing in my ears. Ten thousand Canaanites and Perizzites. Ten thousand Moabites. Six hundred Philistines. Enemies, yes, so why should I care? But I do. The voice never told me how many Israelites died. I do not want to know.

My name is Deborah of Lappidoth. I am a child of Israel, from the hill country of Ephraim. I have had these visions since I was a child. My parents feared them. They feared that I would be called a witch. But they knew my prophecies usually came true. The people of Israel believed in them, too, and they called me Deborah, the Prophetess. I speak for God. I seek the words that God would have me speak, even when they prophesy doom, or when they tell *truth* to the people of Israel—which so often is a message of *doom.* I am Deborah, Woman of Lappidoth. People think Lappidoth is my husband, and as a woman I must be "of" someone. But *lappid* means "torches" in our language, and I am the lighter of torches; whether for worship or for battle, I light the torches that lead the way. It has been many years since our people, the people of Israel, were orphaned in the Land of Canaan by our righteous leaders: first Moses and then Joshua, even Caleb. They assigned each of the tribes of Israel land to conquer, and to hear stories of Joshua's battles, you would think they rid Canaan of every inhabitant. But they did not. They left some of them to dwell among us: Canaanites, Amorites, Amalekites, Hittites, Hivites, Perizzites, Jebusites, and Philistines. Oh, we forced them into slave labor whenever we could get the upper hand, but that didn't last long, and soon "another generation grew up after them, who did not know the Lord or the work that he had done for Israel" (Judg 2:10).

I tried to warn my people. I told them about my vision. An angel appeared and brought these words from God—the same words Joshua told our people: "I brought you up from Egypt, and brought you into the land that I promised to your ancestors. I said, 'I will never break my covenant with you. For your part, do not make a covenant with the inhabitants of this land; tear down their altars'" (Judg 2:1–2). When the people of Israel heard these words, they wept. But they soon forgot. Israel did not break down the altars, they visited them. Israel did not destroy their gods, they worshipped them—their Baals and their Astartes. "The Israelites did what was evil in the sight of the Lord and worshipped the Baals" (Judg 2:11). And we were punished. These people among whom we lived—many of them our distant relatives from the family of Abraham—they became our adversaries. But the Lord who is merciful knew we needed leaders and raised up judges among us. First there was Othniel, son of Caleb's younger brother, who led us for forty peaceful years. Next, we had Ehud for eighty peaceful years, followed briefly by Shamgar, but soon the peace ended. King Jabin of Canaan, with his ruthless army commander, Sisera, and his nine hundred iron chariots have ruled and abused us for twenty years.

A few years ago, my visions returned with a vengeance. I was lighting the torches that led to the tabernacle in Shiloh, and the flames exploded in my head. A voice called out to me: "Deborah, Woman of Lappidoth, I raise you up to be a leader of your people. You will judge according to the Laws of Moses, you will prophesy according to your visions, and you will conquer our adversaries in battle."

I found a place in the hill country of Ephraim, between Ramah and Bethel, where I could see travelers coming and going, on their way north to Shiloh to visit the tabernacle or south to Jerusalem. There I would take my place under a palm tree every day, and they soon called it the Palm of Deborah. People came to me to ask questions and seek my judgements about the laws. Take the commandment, "Thou shall not commit adultery," for instance. One law says if a man rapes a betrothed woman in the countryside—which would be adultery because he has taken another man's betrothed, only the man shall die, because (presumably) the young woman called for help and there was nobody to come to her rescue. But if the rape occurred in the city, both shall die, because (presumably) the woman would have called out if she did not consent to the adultery, and someone (presumably) would have come to her rescue. Many a father of a young woman accused of adultery has come to me begging for the life of his daughter, claiming that the woman could not call out because her rapist's hand was over her mouth, or he had threatened to cut out her tongue if she screamed. Sometimes the responsibility of being judge is too great to bear, but I have been called to bear it.

Today's vision, however, is for Barak—the commander of our army. I have never thought much of Barak, but I think even less of the ruthless Sisera. Both of their faces swirl in my vision, surrounded by flames, dying men, chariots bogged down in the mud, blood flowing in the Wadi Kishon. Barak is there, but where is Sisera? I do not see him. And then I see another face. A woman. I do not know her. She is tending a small flock of sheep near her tent. She stops to mend the tent that is flapping in the breeze. She takes her hammer and pounds the tent peg into the ground to secure it. And then she is gone. The vision ends.

I sent for Barak and said, "'The Lord, the God of Israel, commands you, 'Go, take position at Mount Tabor, bringing ten thousand from the tribe of Naphtali and the tribe of Zebulun. I will draw out Sisera, the general of Jabin's army, to meet you by the river

Kishon with his chariots and his troops; and I will give him into your hand'" (Judg 4:6–7).

Barak stood like a stone pillar before me. His face was as pale as the white clouds that appeared above us. I shook his shoulders and repeated, "God said, 'I will give him into your hand!'" His voice trembled with terror, and he replied, "If you will go with me, I will go, but if you will not go with me, I will not go" (Judg 4:8). The words I uttered next were not my words, but God's words, and the vision of the strange woman at her tent appeared again: "I will surely go with you; nevertheless, the road on which you are going will not lead to your glory, for the Lord will sell Sisera into the hand of a woman" (Judg 4:9). He nodded and smiled weakly. He was happy for me to receive the glory, as long as I accompanied him into battle. But I knew I was not the woman.

We prepared for battle, Barak and I. We summoned the warriors from the tribes of Naphtali and Zebulun to Kedesh. I shouted the battle cry: "Up! For this is the day on which the Lord has given Sisera into your hand. The Lord is indeed going out before you" (Judg 4:14). The warriors answered with one loud voice and charged down from Mount Tabor in their assault on Sisera's army. Miraculously, just as in my vision, I watched as Barak and his ten thousand men were victorious over the army of Sisera. But where is Sisera? Oh, there he is. He has jumped from his chariot and is running away while his army is being slaughtered. What kind of leader does that?

Barak and I had agreed to meet back at the Wadi Kishon if we were separated. Soon a horseman came through our camp shouting, "Sisera is dead! Killed by the woman Jael!" Barak arrived after him and told us the story, and as I heard the words, I remembered my vision. Barak told me what he heard from the woman Jael.

> While abandoning his army, Sisera came upon the tent of Heber the Kenite and his wife, Jael. She was alone at the time, tending her small flock of sheep. Sisera knew there was peace between the house of Heber the Kenite and King Jabin, and he assumed he would find safe haven at the tent of Heber. Jael came out to meet Sisera and said to him, "Turn aside my lord, turn aside to me; have no fear."

> So he turned aside to her into the tent, and she covered him with a rug. Then he said to her, "Please give me a little water to drink, for I am thirsty." So she opened a skin of milk and gave him a drink and covered him. He said to her, "Stand at the door of the tent, and if anyone comes and asks you, 'Is anyone here?' say 'No.'" But Jael, wife of Heber took a tent peg, and took a hammer in her hand, and went softly to him and drove the tent peg into his temple, until it went down into the ground—he was lying fast asleep from weariness—and he died. Then, as [I] Barak came in pursuit of Sisera, Jael went out to meet [me], and said to [me], "Come and I will show you the man whom you are seeking." So [I] went into her tent, and there lay Sisera dead, with the tent peg in his temple. (Judg 4:17–22)

Thousands of men died in battle that day. Thousands more will die before we conquer this land that was promised to us by the Lord, Yahweh. In gratitude, we sing this song of celebration:

> Awake, awake, Deborah! Awake, awake, utter a song!
> Arise, Barak, lead away your captives, O son of Abinoam.
> (Judg 5:12)
>
> The kings came, they fought;
> then fought the kings of Canaan....
> The torrent Kishon swept them away. (Judg 5:19–21)
>
> Most blessed of women be Jael,
> the wife of Heber the Kenite,
> of tent-dwelling women most blessed.
> He asked water and she gave him milk,
> she brought him curds in a lordly bowl.
> She put her hand to the tent peg
> and her right hand to the workmen's mallet;
> she struck Sisera a blow,
> she crushed his head,
> she shattered and pierced his temple,

He sank, he fell,
  he lay still at her feet;
at her feet he sank, he fell;
where he sank, there he fell dead.

Out of the window she peered,
  the mother of Sisera gazed through the lattice:
"Why is his chariot so long in coming?
  Why tarry the hoofbeats of his chariots?"
Her wisest ladies make answer,
  indeed, she answers the question herself:
"Are they not finding and dividing the spoil?—
  A girl or two for every man;
spoil of dyed stuffs for Sisera,
  spoil of dyed stuffs embroidered,
  two pieces of dyed work embroidered for my neck as
    spoil?"

So perish all your enemies, O LORD!
  But may your friends be like the sun as it rises in its might
    (Judg 5:24–31)

Did you notice the difference between the story of Sisera's death that Barak told and the version in the song we now sing after every victory? Barak said Sisera was asleep when Jael drove the tent peg into the ground. The song says he sank and fell at her feet. Which is true? Did Barak miss the cues: the cover, the feet, the empty tent? I sought out the woman, Jael, to give her the glory for conquering Sisera, and she told me the truth as only one woman might tell another.

She was outside her tent tending her small flock of sheep when the general approached her tent. She knew who he was from his battle armor, and from the blood all over his body and the fear in his eyes, she knew he had not been victorious. He demanded that she hide him in her tent. He knew it was not honorable for a man outside the family to enter a woman's tent, but he demanded. Then he demanded water. Then he demanded a cover so he could rest.

And then he demanded her body. He was angry and afraid of his impending death, and he took his anger out on her. She screamed, but there was nobody around to hear her as he abused her, for they were in the countryside. Once satisfied, he sank into a deep sleep. That's when she went outside and got the tent peg and hammer, hid them in her robe, and returned to her tent. She raised Sisera from his sleep as if to seduce him, and then she killed him.

The song is my song. I sang it as a celebration, but I also sang it to honor and protect Jael. I made her a warrior, one who tricked the general with milk and with curds, and then killed him while he stood—warrior to warrior, face to face. It is a violent time we live in. Is there no other way to conquer a group of people but by bloodshed? The people of Israel forget the God who delivered them from Egypt. They prostitute themselves before other gods. They become weak. They fall into the hands of stronger leaders around us, and sometimes it takes years—decades—before they remember God and repent. But God who is merciful is always there with a new leader. How many times will the people of Israel repeat this cycle of disobedience?

Nevertheless, the cycle does repeat, and the people give the same excuses for their bad behavior, saying, "In those days there was no king in Israel; and all the people did what was right in their own eyes" (Judg 21:25). I see it in my visions. It is chaos. I pray for my people and their future. I am Deborah, Woman of Lappidoth.

8
Jephthah's Daughter

Judges 11; Numbers 30; Genesis 22:11–12

I am preparing to walk through the valley of the shadow of death, and I am terrified. I don't know what scares me the most. Will I struggle to be free of the bands that tie me down, or will I faint from fear and never know what happens? If I do not faint, will I feel the blade of the knife as it cuts across my throat? Does the lamb going to slaughter feel pain? Of all the sacrifices that I have witnessed, I have never wondered if the lamb felt pain—until now. Will I be awake as the blood flows from my body? How does it feel to die? What fear will I know during those moments before death? Is it the dying that I fear most, or is it what comes afterward? When I go into the depths of Sheol, will I know I'm there? Will God be there? Will my mother be there? Will I have legs to run to her and arms to wrap around her like I used to when I was a child, and she was alive? Ah, mother, if you were only alive. Would any of this have happened?

What will become of my name? Will my name be cursed as one who died a virgin? God knows, I have mourned my virginity for the last two months. That was one concession my father made—to allow me to go into the hills with my friends to mourn my virginity. Or will I be remembered for my faithfulness? Will they remember how

I adored my father, Jephthah? How I told people over and over that he was one of the greatest judges Israel had ever known? I told them that he would lead our people to battle over the Ammonites, and that he would be victorious, that we would be victorious.

They didn't believe me, but I believed in him. Will they remember that every time he went into battle I prayed for his safety and victory until he returned, and I waited by the window for his return day after day. When he would finally return, I would be there, waiting and praying, ready to run out to greet him. I would dance as I ran to him, my timbrels accompanying my songs of joy. I would leap into his arms, and he would tell me I looked like one from heaven. I would tell him he was Jephthah, the great judge of Israel. How I loved our special greeting. I looked forward to that happy ending after each battle.

Why did he make that oath, my own father? Didn't he know that I would be the first creature he saw when he returned from victory? I was *always* the first one to greet him. Surely the servants would follow, but I was *always* the first one to greet him. I'll never forget his words when he saw me that day. He said, "Alas, my daughter! You have brought me very low; you have become the cause of great trouble to me" (Judg 11:35).

I knew something was wrong the moment I saw his face. It was not the face of a happy victor, not the face I usually saw; it was a face of anguish, of despair. Why had I broken *his* heart? How had I brought trouble on *him*? And then he told me why. He said, "For I have opened my mouth to the Lord, and I cannot take back my vow" (Judg 11:35). How was I to know that he had uttered an oath to God that if he were victorious in battle, "Whoever comes out of the doors of my house to meet me, when I return victorious from the Ammonites, shall be the Lord's to be offered up by me as a burnt offering?" (Judg 11:31). "But you knew, Father," I cried out, "you knew I would be there."

That was it. He had made a vow, and I knew the consequences. In anguish, I cried, "You taught me about vows, Father. You taught me that there is power in the spoken word, especially when it is a vow spoken to God. You told me that vows—both blessings and curses—are so powerful that women cannot be trusted to make them. You told me that the Laws of Moses give a woman's father or husband authority to disapprove of a vow or curse the woman makes, and you told me never to let a vow or curse come from my mouth unless you were there to hear it. Who was there to hear your vow, Father?"

At first, I was more concerned for his life than I was for mine. I feared he would die any moment. He collapsed in sobs in my arms. I held him in that moment of consolation, when he should have been holding me in that moment of victory. I tried to console him. I said, "My father, if you have opened your mouth to the Lord, do to me according to what has gone out of your mouth, now that the Lord has given you vengeance against your enemies, the Ammonites" (Judg 11:36). Will I be remembered for that? Will that be seen as an act of faith, of devotion to my father and my God? Or will it be seen as the consent of one who was disposable—a woman?

In the days that followed, I struggled with many emotions. Fear was paramount. But so were feelings of abandonment, of resentment, of anger. I had to get away. I asked my father to allow me to retreat into the hills with some women I knew—girls, really, about my age. I told him I wanted at least to have some time to mourn my virginity. God knows, I had plenty to mourn. And they mourned with me—for two months. We mourned that my father, the great judge of Israel, made a hasty and irresponsible vow. We mourned that any people—Israelites or Canaanites—would think that God would want them to sacrifice a human being. And we mourned that I would die before being married—would die a virgin—and would not live to see my best friends married, become mothers, become grandmothers. Our fathers and mothers instilled in us that such a death deserved our mourning.

They promised they would not forget me. They promised they would return to the hills and remember me—for four days each year. They promised they would tell their children and grandchildren about me—about my faithfulness—about my bravery. They promised. Some of them tried desperately to persuade me to run away, but I could not. I could run away from my father, perhaps, but I could not run away from God. The oath had been made. God was faithful to my father, and to the people of Israel, and I would be faithful to God. I would return.

And so, I am here. Tomorrow is the day of sacrifice. There is an eerie quiet all around. The servants cry softly every time they see me, and my father will not even look at me. He has not left his room since I returned from the hills. They tell me he has not eaten for days. I fear he will die—from grief if not from guilt.

I am preparing to walk through the valley of the shadow of death, and I am terrified. God, will you be there? Will you speak to my father at the moment he holds the knife to my throat and say what you did to Abraham, long ago on Mt. Moriah? "Abraham, Abraham," you said, "do not lay your hand on the boy or do anything to him; for now I know that you fear God, since you have not withheld your son, your only son, from me" (Gen 22:11–12). Will you provide a ram to be slaughtered in my stead, as you did for my ancestor, Isaac? I, too, am an only child, though not a son, and we, too, fear you—my father and I. Couldn't you speak to my father, and tell him there are other ways for him to fulfill his oath? Couldn't he dedicate me to your service in other ways?

If the answer is no, God, I will be faithful unto death. And I will die believing that you will be with me in Sheol. For you are the great judge; you are my gentle shepherd; you are steadfast love.

9
Hannah

1 Samuel 1—3; Numbers 6:1–21; 30

Have you ever prayed so earnestly that you felt you were really having a conversation with God? Really felt the presence of God? Even heard the voice of God? I had such an experience thirteen years ago.

My name is Hannah, and I live in a tiny village called Ramathaim, in the hill country of Ephraim, about twenty miles from the Great Sea and about thirty miles from Jerusalem. Of course I've never been to any of those places. The only place I've ever been other than my village would be Shiloh. We go there every year to offer sacrifices to God at its shrine. That is where I first heard the voice of God. Being here again this year reminds me of that time.

Let me tell you more about myself. I know that I am a blessed woman, even though I did not always consider myself blessed. I have been married to a wonderful man, Elkanah, for over twenty years. Although I was sure of his love, I couldn't imagine why he would love me. For years, I grieved that I was not fulfilling my duty as a wife. You see, I was barren, and after many years, Elkanah took another wife, Peninah, who gave him many children.

Can you imagine the tension—living in a home with two wives who share one husband? And imagine the pain of the one who has no children. The pain was especially severe when we traveled to

Shiloh each year to offer thanks to God for all our blessings. Each year Elkanah would divide our family offering among us. He did not mean to hurt me, I'm sure, but he made such a show saying, "Here, Peninah, here is your portion. Now bring your sons and daughters so I can give them their portions." That seemed to take forever. And there I stood. Finally, he would come to me, and he would give me a double portion because he loved me so much. Then we would make our offerings to God. He tried to make me feel better, but I did not.

I would feel the stares of the other men and women—especially the women—and imagine their thoughts. "What has she done to lose the favor of the Lord? Why has God closed her womb? Poor child, she has not even one daughter, much less a son. Will she ever be able to redeem herself?" I love God, and I have always tried to live according to God's laws. Even then, I thought God loved me, too, but it was hard not to think as the others thought. Each year that trip made me sick. I would cry constantly and rarely eat throughout our pilgrimage. Dear, kind Elkanah would beg me to come eat with him. "Hannah," he would say, "why do you weep? Why do you not eat? Why is your heart sad? Am I not more to you than ten sons?" (1 Sam 1:8). I just could not help it. I was miserable. I wanted nothing more than to be a mother.

Then came the trip I will never forget. It started as the worst trip of all. At the height of my misery, I went for a walk one night. Weeping uncontrollably, I walked toward the temple of the shrine at Shiloh. Looking up to the heavens and praying aloud, I stumbled and fell, right there on the steps of the shrine of God. There I lay, deep in prayer. I would not have dared enter the temple of the Lord; not me, a woman. I must have looked and sounded crazy.

I cried and prayed for hours. Suddenly, I thought I heard someone call my name. Was I imagining the voice? Was it the voice of the Lord? Would I dare speak directly to God? I did. Not only did I speak but I made a vow. Very quietly, amid sobs, I spoke these words:

> O Lord of hosts, if only you will look on the misery of your servant, and remember me, and not forget your servant, but will give to your servant a male child, then I will set him before you as a nazirite until the day of his death.

He shall drink neither wine nor intoxicants, and no razor shall touch his head. (1 Sam 1:11)

I waited to be struck dead, or at least to be chastised by someone. You see, in my culture, a woman's vow can be revoked by her husband (or father if she is not married, or even her son), and I was being reckless—if not offensive to God—for making a vow on my own, with no husband around even to consider revoking it! (see Num 30).

I looked up to see if anyone had heard the words I had just blurted out, and I heard myself gasp in surprise. There was Eli, the high priest, sitting on the seat beside the door of the temple. I must admit, what he said next did not frighten me; instead, I had to stifle my laughter. He asked if I was drunk! I can understand how I must have appeared, but I assured him that I was not drunk. "I am a woman deeply troubled," I said, "I have drunk neither wine nor strong drink, but I have been pouring out my soul before the LORD" (1 Sam 1:15).

I looked into his eyes, and I saw great sadness and sincere sympathy. I was confused; it seemed as though he shared my anguish. But why? He had sons. All he said was, "Go in peace; the God of Israel grant the petition you have made to him" (1 Sam 1:17). And he slipped away quietly in the darkness of the night.

That was the turning point in my life. I had asked God for much and had promised much, but when Eli said, "Go in peace," I knew that *peace* was really what I wanted. I was a new woman, no longer miserable, but at peace with God and at peace with myself—even at peace with Peninah!

If my story had ended there, I would still be at peace, but it got better. The next year—by now an old woman, by most accounts—I had a son! I named him Samuel. But I knew he did not really belong to me or to Elkanah. He belonged to God. I finally explained my vow to Elkanah, and he agreed to my plan for Samuel, once he was weaned. When he was about three years old, we took him with us to Shiloh and brought him to Eli. I told Eli about my vow, and he remembered me. I said, "For this child I prayed; and the LORD has granted me the petition that I made to him. Therefore, I have lent him to the LORD; as long as he lives, he is given to the LORD" (1 Sam 1:27–28).

I left my precious baby with the priest to serve the Lord all of his life. Please do not think I am a bad mother for giving my son up to Eli; I was only returning him to God. Oh, I missed him greatly, and I could not wait for each year to pass when we would return to Shiloh for the sacrifice. I would visit Samuel and bring him a new robe. We would sit and talk. I would tell him stories about God, and he would tell me stories about Shiloh.

Samuel felt privileged to help old Eli and to sleep in the very temple of the Lord that held the Ark of the Covenant. And it seemed that almost every other year I would bring a new brother or sister for him to meet—I had three sons and two daughters after Samuel. And now Samuel is twelve years old.

Even as a little boy, Samuel seemed to know so much about God. Do you know special children like that? I remember once when he was four years old, he said, "Mother, does God still talk to people today as in the days of Abraham and Moses?" I said, "I do not know, Samuel, what do you think?" He looked up at me with his big, brown eyes and said, "I think so, Mother. I think God spoke to me last night as I was falling asleep." "What did God say?" I asked. With the simple faith of a child, he replied, "God said, 'I love you, Samuel.'"

Samuel was very dear to Eli; as it turned out, Eli's sons were scoundrels. Eli did not seem to me to be particularly close to God, and his sons—oh, the stories Samuel told me about his sons! When he got a little older, he figured out what Eli's sons were doing with women—right there at the entrance to the shrine at Shiloh! Samuel said nobody at the shrine really talked much about God. They even stole the sacrifices and gifts the people brought to give to God.

Samuel knew that I had promised him to God, and as he got older, I knew there would come a time when he accepted God's will for his life. I discovered just today while talking to my dear son that that time has come. Last night, Samuel was sleeping in the room near the ark of God, when he heard a voice call his name: "Samuel, Samuel." He thought it was Eli, and he ran over to where Eli was sleeping and said, "Here I am." But it was not Eli; in fact, Eli told him to go back and lie down. And then he heard the voice call his name again—only this time he was wide awake! Again, he went to Eli, and again Eli told him to lie down.

The third time Samuel heard his name and went to Eli, something must have told Eli that it was the Lord calling Samuel, so he said, "Go, lie down; and if he calls you, you shall say, 'Speak, Lord, for your servant is listening'" (1 Sam 3:9). Samuel told me that he did just what Eli said to do, and lo and behold, the Lord God spoke to Samuel and told him what was going to happen to Eli and his sons as punishment for their sins. Poor little Samuel. He was scared to tell Eli what God said, so he just lay there all night until this morning when Eli insisted that Samuel tell him what God said. I think Eli knew it was bad.

I do not think Eli or anyone else around here has heard the voice of God in years, only my little Samuel. I thank God that I was here today to comfort him. I know God will continue to speak to him, and I hope he continues to listen. Praise to the Lord, the Almighty, the King of Creation!

10
Michal

1 Samuel 8—12; 18—19; 25; 2 Samuel 3—6

Did you see him? There in the street below the palace, leaping and dancing and exposing himself for everyone to see. Did you see him? I did, and I was disgusted. I told him so. But who am I? I am no longer Michal, daughter of Saul. Saul is dead. I am no longer even Michal, wife of David, for he has forsaken me. I am only a small part of a complex game, a desperate and vicious battle for the throne, not just to be a king, but to be *the* king of Israel.

My father, Saul, was the first king of Israel, but some say the weight of responsibility drove him to madness. He was not an evil man, and he wanted the best for the people we call Israelites. But some of them turned against him, and they told him that God had turned against him—the same God who told the prophet Samuel to anoint my father as the first king of Israel.

I have been told many stories about Samuel, my father, and my husband, David. Some of these stories followed them from battle, but I have my doubts about the stories soldiers tell. Isn't it interesting that the one who tells the story is always the bravest and has killed more enemies than anyone else? I don't understand the glory in killing—even killing done in the name of the Lord. Where is the glory in slaughtering women and children, or slaughtering their husbands and fathers and leaving them helpless? Where is the glory in burning their fields and their flocks?

My father, Saul, was born at a time of great despair for our people, the Israelites. We have been in this land, our Promised Land, for more than two hundred years. After Moses and then Joshua, God sent us judges—some good, some bad. Samuel was a good one, but his sons were no better than those of Eli, the priest of the tabernacle. At one point it was so bad that God left us, or at least that's what our elders said when the Ark of the Covenant fell into the hands of our enemies, the Philistines.

And so, our people begged Samuel to appoint a king so we could be strong and powerful like the enemies who threatened us. But Samuel warned them against their desire for a king. He told us a king would rule over us, conscript our sons and daughters to his service, take our land and harvests, and then take a tenth of whatever we produce.

I think Samuel was trying to tell us that God is our only king, the only one who deserves the first fruits of our labors, the only one who deserves our allegiance. After Samuel proclaimed my father king, he gave one last warning. He said if the king and his people fail to follow the Lord, "then the hand of the Lord will turn against you and your king" (1 Sam 12:15). And it did.

My father was the first one to hold that dangerous position of king. He was the tallest and most handsome of the men, and humble—at least in his early years. In fact, I've heard stories about how he was chosen by the casting of lots, and when Samuel called for him, he was hiding among the baggage. Like Moses, he didn't think he was ready for the role. He was a true soldier, successful in battle, and his enemies feared him. Even the Philistines. We loved him: my brothers Jonathan, Ishvi, and Malchishua; my sister Merab; and our mother, Ahinoam. In my childhood memories he is still the tallest, bravest, and most handsome of men.

I heard the stories whispered throughout the House of Saul, too, stories that said God was angry with my father because he did not follow the laws about taking spoils of war, or that he thought more about himself than God. They said God told Samuel he was sorry he ever chose my father to be king. They said God told Samuel to find another king. That king was David.

David! Oh, how well I remember the first time I saw him. He was so beautiful. Not handsome, beautiful. His hair curled around his face, and he was brave and strong, faithful and humble. Where did that man go?

I knew of David before I ever saw him. After all, he was the one who slew the champion Goliath, the Philistine of Gath. Killed him with only a sling and a rock! My brother Jonathan admired David and urged us to come to the rooftop and peer through the walls to see his triumphal entry below. We heard the people shout, "Saul has killed his thousands, and David his ten thousands" (1 Sam 18:7). My father was jealous, furious. And the more David endeared himself to the people, the more our father wanted him gone, even dead.

This is where Merab and I enter the picture. This is my story, a painful story of love and hate, of promise and betrayal.

You see, our father, Saul, used us to get rid of David. First, Merab. He promised her to David in exchange for fighting the Philistines. She was so excited, and I was happy for her. But then with no explanation at all "she was given to Adriel the Meholathite as a wife" (1 Sam 18:19).

Merab was devoted to duty over love; she was a dutiful daughter and a dutiful wife, and she now loves Adriel. She even forgave our father. Not me. I loved David even more, after Merab was given to Adriel. Everyone knew that, and they told our father, who seemed pleased. I should have known not to trust him. Knowing David could pay no bride price, my father agreed to give me to him in exchange for one hundred Philistine foreskins, expecting David's certain death in the process of acquiring them.

Was that necessary? It's true, he was a shepherd, but not a hired laborer. He was the youngest son of his father Jesse, a landowner. Did he truly have no bride price? Or was he as manipulative as my father, King Saul? I was terrified for him when he set out to battle. I waited anxiously for his return. And he did! He returned not with one hundred but with two hundred Philistine foreskins, and I became his wife. I am certain this only added to my father's fury, which was intense and unpredictable. People said he had an evil spirit from God, but I didn't know what to think.

And me? In spite of my love for David, I drowned in guilt. Oh, I was happy to become his wife, but I grieved that my good fortune came with the destruction of two hundred families. And I knew my good fortune was not to last long. In spite of David's efforts to serve my father, and in spite of Jonathan's efforts to appeal to our father on his behalf, our father, King Saul, was determined to kill my new husband.

One night, I looked out the window of our house, and I saw men—my father's men—creeping around our house, and I told David he should leave. He did not want to leave me; he was not afraid. He was a genuine man of God—then—and he urged me to join him in prayer. He prayed, "The Lord is my shepherd; I shall not want....Even though I walk through the darkest valley, I fear no evil; for you are with me" (Ps 23:1, 4).

I don't have the same faith in the God of Israel that my husband has. That God has never proven faithful to me. That God declared me property, first of my father and then of my husband. That God told my father to kill innocent men, women, and children. At least, that's what they told me. I preferred to put my hope in the gods of the Canaanites, much to the dismay of my father and husband. In fact, when I finally convinced David to escape by climbing down out of the window, I took one of my household gods and placed it in our bed, covering it with David's clothes. I even placed a skin with goat's hair on the top of the image and placed covers over it.

Just as I expected, soon I heard the voices of my father's men, as they burst through our door, demanding to see David. I sent them away, with news that he was ill. That was not proof enough for my father, and he sent the men back, demanding they bring my husband to him—even if they had to bring the bed with him in it. When they discovered my lie, they took me to my father, and I witnessed his fury, the evil spirit I had heard about. Fearing for my own life, and fearing I may never see my beloved again, I lied again. I told my father that David threatened to kill me if I did not help him escape.

Years passed; the fighting continued. Though a renegade in my father's eyes, David became more powerful, and my father, King

Saul, lost power. Our people loved David. Like most men, David took two more wives: Abigail, widow of Nabal, and Ahinoam of Jezreel. I remained faithful to David, even though I knew I might never see him again. My father, Saul, had no use for me now, and I guess he never forgave me for turning against him, so he gave me—*gave me*—to another man, Palti the son of Laish, who was of Gallim.

Dear Palti—I called him Paltiel—he was like a father to me, and his wife welcomed me into their home. I think Paltiel is the only man from whom I have ever known true love. He loved me for who I was, not *whose* I was, or what I had, for I had nothing. Nobody knows what happened during my years with Paltiel, but I will tell you. I cared for his wife when she became ill and died, but he never *took* me for his wife. He knew I was saving myself for David. I was sure David would soon return for me, but he did not, and eventually I became accustomed to my new life in Gallim.

War raged between the Israelites—under the leadership of King Saul—and the Philistines, and one day, word came to us that my father and brothers, Jonathan and Malchishua, had died on Mount Gilboa. I mourned their deaths, especially my brothers'.

Time passed and the House of Saul was at war against the House of David. And then one day, messengers came with news that David was poised to be king over all of Israel. He had made a covenant with Abner, Saul's general, who was feared even by Saul's son Ishbosheth, and now they were coming to take me away from Paltiel, to take me back to David. I heard that David reminded Abner about those two hundred Philistine foreskins—the *price* he paid for me. Did he still love me? I wondered. Did I want him to love me, after all this? I feared that he didn't love me, he only wanted some connection—any connection—to the House of Saul so he could make claim to the throne of Israel.

By that time, he had six other wives and many sons and daughters, and he had the admiration of his people and my father's people; why did he need me? I will never forget the day they took me back to David. Poor Paltiel followed us, weeping, "all the way to Bahurim" (2 Sam 3:16). I wept too. Finally, when we reached Bahurim, Abner said he had heard enough. He shouted to Paltiel to return to Gallim, and finally he did. I never saw him again.

I never saw David again either—face to face, that is, until today. Oh, I saw him as he moved around from wife to wife. And I saw him as he rode through the city gates, the city he called the City of David, on his way to and from battle. But he never called for me. I had saved myself for him, and he never called for me. I was thinking of this today when I heard the commotion in the streets below—people shouting and the sound of the ram's horn. I looked out and saw *the Great King David,* wearing only a linen ephod, "leaping and dancing before the LORD" like an ecstatic priest, and I "despised him in [my] heart" (2 Sam 6:16).

Later he entered his great house with typical fanfare and called for his wives to come greet him and receive his blessing. I couldn't help myself. As he passed by each of us, I confronted him: "How the king of Israel honored himself today, uncovering himself today before the eyes of his servants' maids, as one of the vulgar fellows shamelessly uncovers himself" (2 Sam 6:20). He looked at me with eyes void of love, void of emotion and sneered:

> It was before the LORD, who chose me in place of your father and all his household, to appoint me a prince over Israel, the people of the LORD, that I have danced before the LORD. I will make myself yet more contemptible than this, and I will be abased in my own eyes; but by the maids of whom you have spoken, by them I shall be held in honor. (2 Sam 6:21–22)

As he walked away, I thought, "Have them, damn you. Have them all. Have one thousand of them and see what misery they bring you. I loved you, David. I loved you before you were king, and I would have helped you be a good king. Not now. I never want to see you again. I would rather die childless than have you ever touch me again." And then I knew I had prophesied my own destiny: I would die childless. He did not need me. My father used me. My husband used me. And now, I was useless. Worthless. Worth less than all his women. Michal, daughter of Saul; Michal, sister of Jonathan; Michal, wife of David; Michal.

11
Abigail

1 Samuel 25; 2 Samuel 3:2–5

I am not yet a mother, and I am already a widow. I am a widow, and I am a murderer. I killed my own husband. I know I did. They tried to convince me I did not, but I saw the look in his eyes the moment he was struck with whatever evil spirit possessed him—an evil spirit brought upon him by his rage, which was brought upon him by me. Some physicians don't believe in evil spirits; they said his heart died within him, but I know it was my fault. I sat by his side for ten days as the breath left his body, a little at a time until he was as hard as the stone that killed the giant, Goliath. I carry with me a guilt that will never be assuaged: bloodguilt.

My name is Abigail. My name means "my father's joy." My mother told me how proud my father was when I was born, his first-born child. He did not mourn that I was not a son. All my life I knew that I was special to my father. He taught me to be bold, to be strong, to be decisive. I am like my father in many ways, and like him, I have a good intuition about people. I always have. Except with Nabal. My father warned me, but I didn't listen. He was rich, and I wanted the life he promised me, so I married him.

Nabal. What parent would name a child Nabal? It means "fool"! In my culture, a "nabal" is a glutton, a miser, a stupid, mean-spirited person who has no respect or love for God. That was my husband,

Nabal. Oh, he was rich, with vast lands in Carmel. He owned three thousand sheep, one thousand goats, and fertile land enough to support his flocks. I would often ride out on my little donkey to deliver refreshment to the men and women who tended our flocks, and I marveled at the grandeur of our lands—even the desert lands.

I loved my daily tasks: several hours to prepare, several hours to deliver supplies, several hours to return home, and many hours away from the man who lived up to his name. One day my tasks took even longer than usual. It was sheep-shearing time, a happy time for all of us, because our wealth increased by virtue of our flock. As I returned to our home, one of my husband's servants came running to meet me. Breathlessly, he told me what had happened in my absence. Ten strange men had arrived, announcing that they came in the name of David, slayer of Goliath, warrior of the House of Judah.

I have heard of this David. They say he has slain tens of thousands of Philistines, amassed an army of six hundred men, and has gone from village to village with his trademark tactics: threaten, then negotiate for alliances—even with the Philistines. They say that the prophet Samuel anointed him King of Israel—this same prophet who earlier anointed Saul the king of Israel. Samuel had just died, and like all of Israel, we mourned him. There seemed to be no end to fighting. Israel against the Philistines, Judah against the Amalekites, the House of Saul against the House of David. Did the Lord our God truly choose David over Saul?

The servant told me that David's men greeted Nabal warmly, saying, "Peace be to you, and peace be to your house, and peace be to all that you have" (1 Sam 25:6). They brought this message from David:

> I hear that you have shearers; now your shepherds have been with us, and we did them no harm, and they missed nothing, all the time they were in Carmel. Ask your young men, and they will tell you. Therefore let my young men find favor in your sight; for we have come on a feast day. Please give whatever you have at hand to your servants and to your son David. (1 Sam 25:7–8)

Our servants insisted David's men were telling the truth. According to our servants, David sent messengers out of the wilderness to salute our master, and our master shouted insults at them. Yet the men were very good to us, and we suffered no harm, and we never missed anything when we were in the fields, as long as we were with them; they were a wall to us both by night and by day, all the while we were with them keeping the sheep (1 Sam 25:15–16).

They came in peace, but Nabal thought them to be dishonest, that it was a ploy to gain his favor and then take advantage of him at sheep-shearing time. Foolish man! Instead of extending hospitality to them, he mocked them and insulted them. He said:

> Who is David? Who is the son of Jesse? There are many servants today who are breaking away from their masters. Shall I take my bread and my water and the meat that I have butchered for my shearers, and give it to men who come from I do not know where? (1 Sam 25:10–11)

I could see the fear in the young servant's eyes. He said, "They could have come with swords, but they came with blessings." He pleaded with me, "Now therefore know this and consider what you should do; for evil has been decided against our master and against all his house; he is so ill-natured that no one can speak to him" (1 Sam 25:17). It was clear that many had already tried to reason with him to no avail.

I could just imagine my Nabal, my stupid, mean-spirited husband, responding like that to the men who had protected our people. Like my father would have done, I went right to work. I ran into the house and instructed the maids to fire the ovens—even though it was the heat of the day and the bread had already been baked. I told them we were doing this to protect our lands, our homes, our families, our very lives. We prepared two hundred loaves of bread, and we packed some of the delicacies that had been prepared for the merriment that was to follow the sheep shearing: "two skins of wine, five sheep ready dressed, five measures of parched grain, one hundred clusters of raisins, and two hundred cakes of figs" (1 Sam 25:18). The servants helped me carry the supplies surreptitiously from the storehouses, right under the nose of the fool, Nabal. They helped me load them onto donkeys, and off they went to the camp of David. I waited a few minutes and then followed on my own donkey, as if I were setting off to deliver supplies to our shepherds.

We rode quietly into the camp of David, and as I slid carefully off my donkey and peered over the mountain ravine, I heard David say to his men:

> Surely it was in vain that I protected all that this fellow has in the wilderness, so that nothing was missed of all that belonged to him; but he has returned me evil for good. God do so to David and more also, if by morning I leave so much as one male of all who belong to him. (1 Sam 25:21)

Oh no! Was I too late?

Remembering my father's encouragement to be bold and strong, I walked confidently to David, bowed as if he were my king, and then fell prostrate at his feet. I hadn't planned my speech, but the words came with as much deference as I could possibly convey:

> Upon me alone, my lord, be the guilt; please let your servant speak in your ears, and hear the words of your servant. My lord, do not take seriously this ill-natured fellow, Nabal; for as his name is, so is he; Nabal is his name, and folly is with him; but I, your servant, did not see the young men of my lord, whom you sent.
>
> Now then, my lord, as the Lord lives, and as you yourself live, since the Lord has restrained you from bloodguilt and from taking vengeance with your own hand, now let your enemies and those who seek to do evil to my lord be like Nabal. And now let this present that your servant has brought to my lord be given to the young men who follow my lord. (1 Sam 25:24–27)

The words continued, as if I were a prophet sent from God:

> Please forgive the trespass of your servant; for the Lord will certainly make my lord a sure house, because my

> lord is fighting the battles of the LORD; and evil shall not be found in you so long as you live. If anyone should rise up to pursue you and to seek your life, the life of my lord shall be bound in the bundle of the living under the care of the LORD your God; but the lives of your enemies he shall sling out as from the hollow of a sling. When the LORD has done to my lord according to all the good that he has spoken concerning you, and has appointed you prince over Israel, my lord shall have no cause of grief, or pangs of conscience, for having shed blood without cause or for having saved himself. And when the LORD has dealt well with my lord, then remember your servant. (1 Sam 25:28–31)

I hadn't really looked at him closely while pleading with him. I only saw his dusty sandals and the hem of his robe—dry feet and tattered robe that spoke of his difficult journeys and hard-fought battles. And then he took me by the hand and brought me to my feet, and I saw how beautiful he was. Looking into my eyes, he said:

> Blessed be the LORD, the God of Israel, who sent you to meet me today. Blessed be your good sense, and blessed be you, who have kept me today from bloodguilt and from avenging myself by my own hand! For as surely as the LORD the God of Israel lives, who has restrained me from hurting you, unless you had hurried and come to meet me, truly by morning there would not have been left to Nabal so much as one male. (1 Sam 25:32–34)

Perhaps I was not too late after all! I had offered a way to prevent him from incurring bloodguilt!

My servants and I extended the hand of hospitality to David's warriors, serving them the bread, fig cakes, wine, and other provisions. When the men had finished, David offered his blessing: "Go up to your house in peace; see, I have heeded your voice, and I have granted your petition" (1 Sam 25:35). And then we left.

Who was this man who inspired his troops to go to battle with little armor, to live in caves and in the desert with little to eat, who offered words of peace where my foolish husband offered only words of hatred? I wanted to know more about him. But for now, I had to face another man: my Nabal. When I arrived at home it was nighttime, and my husband was holding a banquet fit for a king. He had no idea what it meant to be a king, but I had just met one who did.

Nabal was drunk with wine and merriment, and I thought it was not a good time to tell him what I did, so I went to my bed and slept, dreaming of the beautiful warrior who spoke words of peace. I awoke the next morning to see the face of my Nabal, darkness under his eyes from too much wine. I told him what I did. I told him that I saved him and our household from the swords of David and his men. I told him of the beautiful, mighty David. Suddenly his eyes opened wider than I had ever seen them, and he clutched his chest in pain and fell across the bed. Ten days later, he was dead.

If I'd had a chance to mourn his death, would I have done so? I will never know. As the sounds of wailing echoed from our household, we heard footsteps outside. It was David's men. Had they come to kill us after all? I ran to the gate and fell at their feet, pleading: "Please do not bring harm upon my household. My husband, Nabal is dead." The leader of the soldiers took me by the hand and said, "David has sent us to you to take you to him as his wife" (1 Sam 25:40).

What could I say? I was a widow, and for all I knew, I would be called a murderer. My Nabal, my foolish husband was dead, and another man—wise and courageous—wanted me for a wife. Should I leave the comfort and wealth of Carmel and follow one who lived in caves and depended on others for his food? Did I believe my words from the previous day were from God or simply the pleading of a desperate woman? Did I believe the House of David would be a lasting dynasty? I bowed low to the messenger and said, "Your servant is a slave to wash the feet of the servants of my lord" (1 Sam 25:41).

David took me for his wife, and with me he acquired my husband's land and flocks and wealth. Of course that's why he wanted me! I soon learned I was not his first. One of the soldiers told me of Michal, daughter of Saul, who became his wife for the bride price of one hundred Philistine foreskins. I heard how she protected him from the wrath of King Saul. I wondered what happened to her after David broke with Saul.

Soon I welcomed another sister-wife, Ahinoam of Jezreel. Today Ahinoam and I set out in a caravan to go to the land of Gath, where David found refuge with King Achish, who gave him the city of Ziklag. He says he will take Hebron next. I wonder: Who will deliver the first child for David? Will we have daughters or sons?

Am I already with child? If I have a son, what will I name him? I think I will name him Chileab. This Hebrew name has many meanings. I've heard it means "Like his father," but it also means "Restraint of the father." I pray that his father is David, and he will be like him, beautiful and acting with restraint. If his father is Nabal, I would not question God for taking him before he is old enough to cause harm to David and our people.

Ahinoam and I will serve our king, David, and we will help him secure the allegiance of Judah and Israel. How clever he was to choose as wives Abigail the Carmelite and Ahinoam the Jezreelite. We are from Judah, and with our marriages, he claimed the Carmelites, Calebites, and Jezreelites. But this clever man hopes there are many fools in Israel who will think of Mt. Carmel and the Valley of Jezreel in the north when they think of David's wives, for he wants to unite all the tribes of Israel, north and south, into one kingdom, the Kingdom of David.

We, Ahinoam and I, will be companions on this strange journey, joined by who knows how many other women, all following this beautiful man who sings the songs of our ancestors:

> Let all the earth fear the Lord; let all the inhabitants of the world stand in awe of him.
> For he spoke, and it came to be; he commanded, and it stood firm. (Ps 33:8–9)

12
Bathsheba

2 Samuel 11—12; 1 Kings 1—2

The great King David lay upon what would surely be his death bed. Nathan, the king's prophet, urged me to go to him, and so I went. Lying close to him—they *said* to keep him warm—was the sweet, young Shunammite virgin, Abishag. Like one of his servants, I bowed to him, then I looked him in the eyes and said three words, "You promised me." He knew what I meant.

My name is Bathsheba. I am one of the king's wives, the mother of Solomon. The king promised that my son would succeed him as king. And I am determined to see that he fulfills his promise, or else I will take matters into my own hands. I promise.

My story began many years ago. I was the wife of Uriah, the Hittite. It was spring, and Uriah was fighting with all of Israel against the Ammonites while their great commander, King David, remained behind in Jerusalem in his palace, gazing out over the rooftops of the city below. I had just completed my period of monthly impurity, and I was observing the law of the ritual cleansing bath on the rooftop of my house, on one of the terraces below the palace of the king. Before I had completed the ritual, I heard a knock on the door of my house, and I quickly dressed and went to the door. I was surprised to see a messenger from the king.

At first my heart sank. I feared that they came with word of my husband Uriah's death, but what they said surprised me out of my fear. They said the king wanted to see me. Why? But what could I do? I could not refuse the king. I followed the messengers to the palace. To my great surprise, they took me to the private quarters of the king and quickly departed.

As soon as the doors closed behind me, the king pulled me to his bed and raped me. I tried to stop him. But he raped me anyway. And then he sent me home. What would I tell Uriah? I could not tell him anything. I was his wife, and I had been defiled. He had been defiled. But Uriah couldn't bring charges against his king!

If that were not enough, the unthinkable happened. Several weeks later, the way of women did not come upon me. I was pregnant, and Uriah had still not returned. If my husband returned and found me pregnant, he would accuse me of adultery, and I would be stoned to death! Not knowing what to do, I sent word to the king. Surely the wise king David would know what to do. But imagine my surprise when, a few days later, Uriah returned to Jerusalem! He told me that the king had inquired about the war and told him, "Go down to your house, and wash your feet" (2 Sam 11:8). Aha, so that was his plan. He wanted Uriah to "wash his feet" (to lie with me) to cover up his sin! But my husband, my honorable husband, refused to sleep in our bed. Instead, he slept outside—and this is what he said to the king:

> The ark and Israel and Judah remain in booths; and my lord Joab and the servants of my lord are camping in the open field; shall I then go to my house, to eat and to drink, and to lie with my wife? As you live, and as your soul lives, I will not do such a thing. (2 Sam 11:11)

Such a good man, my husband Uriah.

The next day the king invited my husband to dine with him, and he gave him strong drink. Did he hope to arouse him so that he would sleep with me? But alas, he slept with the king's servants and did not return to our house. What could I say to him? Nothing. The next day he returned to battle, sending his love to me by a messenger.

Soon I learned that the army of Joab had suffered heavy casualties in battle, and messengers arrived with the news that my husband had been killed in battle. I pressed them for information, and they said that the reports were confusing, that somehow my husband had been sent to the front lines, and when the battle grew intense, the army drew back from him, leaving him exposed to the archers on the walls of the city. I remember thinking, "Why would they leave him exposed?"

My head swirled, my stomach wretched, and I fell to the ground. When I awoke, my mother was there comforting me, and she took me to my bed to rest and to grieve. I grieved for a month, as is our custom, and I soon realized that I was not the only one counting the days. At the end of the month, the king sent for me and took me to his palace. He took me for his wife, but he told everyone he only wanted to care for the widow of his loyal servant, Uriah.

In due course, I gave birth to a son. He was beautiful, like his father, David, but he was weak. Was this God's punishment for our sin? His father, the king, came to see us. He was noticeably moved to see his son near death. Was this grief or guilt? He promised to fast and pray for him to live. But after seven days, our precious son died. I grieved—for my son, for my husband Uriah, for the future that was unpredictable, for the way of women. And my husband, the king, as soon as he learned his son had died, bathed, changed his clothes, and went into the House of the Lord (2 Sam 12:20).

Did he pray for forgiveness? Did he pray for another son? A few days later he came to console me. He promised he would give me another son. He promised me my son would be the next king. And then he lay with me. His promises flowed with his seed, and soon I knew I was again with child. I gave birth to a son and named him Solomon.

You may think this is the end of my story, but it is just the beginning. Years passed. Solomon grew to be a strong prince and a promising warrior. David's own son Absalom killed his own brother Amnon as revenge for raping his sister Tamar. What a tragic family this is! Absalom then conspired against his own father, mounting a rebellion against the throne. When word came to the king, David so feared the advance of Absalom that he took all of us and fled

Jerusalem, leaving only ten concubines behind. I've never seen him more disconsolate. We all covered our heads and wept as we left Jerusalem. We paused and looked back at the beautiful City of David, and our king David led us to the Mount of Olives, barefoot and heads covered, weeping all the way (2 Sam 15).

The battles that had raged in the days of King Saul continued through the days of King David. Absalom died in battle. David returned to Jerusalem. Many years passed, and the great King David became old and feeble. His first son Amnon was dead, murdered by his second son Absalom, also dead. His third son Chileab died young, and the fourth son Adonijah is now a man, as is my son Solomon. There are many more sons and daughters, but all that matters to me now is Solomon.

Just recently, Adonijah, son of Haggith, was heard saying, "I will be king" (1 Kgs 1:5). In fact, I learned he is preparing a banquet to celebrate. He has already established his royal court: Joab as commander of the army and Abiathar as priest, but he did not invite the king's prophet Nathan or Benaiah the priest. Nathan is the one who told me, "Have you not heard that Adonijah son of Haggith has become king and our lord David does not know it?" (1 Kgs 1:11). I was horrified to hear this! How could it be? He promised me!

Nathan advised me:

> Now therefore come, let me give you advice, so that you may save your own life and the life of your son Solomon. Go in at once to King David and say to him, "Did you not, my lord the king, swear to your servant, saying: Your son Solomon shall succeed me as king, and he shall sit on my throne? Why then is Adonijah king?" Then while you are still there speaking with the king, I will come in after you and confirm your words. (1 Kgs 1:12–14)

And so, I did as the prophet advised. I told my husband, King David:

> Adonijah has become king, though you, my lord the king, do not know it. He has sacrificed oxen, fatted cattle, and sheep in abundance, and has invited all the children of

> the king, the priest Abiathar, and Joab the commander of the army; but your servant Solomon he has not invited. But you, my lord the king—the eyes of all Israel are on you to tell them who shall sit on the throne of my lord the king after him. Otherwise it will come to pass, when my lord the king sleeps with his ancestors, that my son Solomon and I will be counted offenders. (1 Kgs 1:18–21)

While I was speaking, Nathan entered and confirmed all that I said. The king called me to him and said:

> As the Lord lives, who has saved my life from every adversity, as I swore to you by the Lord, the God of Israel, "Your son Solomon shall succeed me as king, and he shall sit on my throne in my place," so will I do this day. (1 Kgs 1:29–30)

I bowed low with my face to the ground and said, "May my lord King David live forever!" (1 Kgs 1:31). He summoned the priest Zadok, the prophet Nathan, and Benaiah and instructed them to anoint Solomon king over Israel. They did as he instructed, and they blew the trumpet as Solomon rode into Jerusalem on the king's mule, with the people shouting, "Long live King Solomon" (1 Kgs 1:39). Soon Adonijah and his guests heard the news, and they ran away from the banquet in fear. Solomon sent for Adonijah and heard his plea for the new king to spare his life. He allowed him to go home, and he said he would spare his life as long as he didn't do anything wicked, but I don't think that promise will last very long. I'm sure Solomon will find a way to make sure Adonijah cannot try to seize the throne.

My son is now king. My husband kept his promise. He will likely die soon. Will my son reign in peace? Will he be a wise king, or will he be consumed by the quest for power that consumed his father? Will he be satisfied with one wife, or two or three, or will he need one thousand wives to secure his kingdom? I pray to the God of Abraham that he will:

Be strong, be courageous, and keep the charge of the LORD [our] God, walking in his ways and keeping his statutes, his commandments, his ordinances, and his testimonies, as it is written in the law of Moses, so that [he] can prosper in all that [he does] and wherever he turns. (1 Kgs 2:2–3)

13
Tamar, Daughter of David

2 Samuel 5—8; 13

He raped me. My own brother raped me. And I will tell you this: Rape has nothing to do with sex. It's about power. Everything around me smells—no, it stinks—of power and the tragic trail of sadness and death that comes from the struggle for power, even in a family.

My name is Tamar. I am a princess, the daughter of King David. My mother is Maacah, his third wife—well, fourth if you count Michal. My brother, Absalom, is also a son of David by our mother, Maacah, but we have other brothers and sisters. Well, the truth is we have many half-brothers and sisters through our father's multiple wives and concubines, and every one of them has a wish—and a plan—to become the king's heir. Oh my, this is such a complicated story. Where do I begin?

Let me start with the happy days. When were they? To be honest, I was the happiest as a little girl in Hebron. There were several of us then, happy little children who shared several mothers and one father: David. My favorite mothers were Abigail, Ahinoam, and of course Maacah, mother of my brother Absalom and me. The two of us loved playing with our brothers, especially Amnon and Chileab. We were brokenhearted when Chileab died at a young age. We adored our father, David, and when he marched into the town of Hebron, he was like a king coming home with his army. I was so young, but I can see and hear and smell the memories. I didn't understand the politics then. Now I understand better.

You see, my father was on a quest—a quest to unite the twelve tribes of the Hebrew people into a unified kingdom: Israel. Many people already called him king and had followed him even since his days in the court of King Saul and in his years as a renegade and a mercenary, but he wanted to secure the allegiance of the Hebrews from Dan to Beersheba. After seven years in Hebron, he made a shrewd decision; he established the City of David in Jerusalem. Zion was a city that had sacred meaning to Hebrews, but was impartial to the northern or southern tribes.

I remember when we packed our belongings and traveled in a long caravan from Hebron to Jerusalem. By this time my father had thirty thousand men who came with him, along with their wives and children. And he had—for the first time in the history of our people—an organized administration: Joab was leader of the army; Jehoshaphat, recorder; Zadok and Ahimelech, priests; Seriah, secretary; and Benaiah, who was over the Kerethites and Pelethites.

He even appointed his sons as priests. When we arrived, they had already begun to build up the palace from the terraces inward, and oh, it was impressive! King Hiram of Tyre had sent poles of cedar that smelled so fragrant, and he sent carpenters and stonemasons to build the fortress and palace. I remember the prayer my father prayed when he called the priests to bless his new palace:

> And now, O Lord God, you are God, and your words are true, and you have promised this good thing to your servant; now therefore may it please you to bless the house of your servant, so that it may continue forever before you; for you, O Lord God, have spoken, and with your blessing shall the house of your servant be blessed forever. (2 Sam 7:28–29)

In Jerusalem, my father took more wives and concubines, and many more sons and daughters were added to our family, but as my brothers Amnon and Absalom began to reach manhood, they spent more time learning to be warriors and princes and had little time to play with me. They even received their own houses—separate rooms in the now sprawling palace of the king. I stayed with the women of the palace, and as I got older, I was not allowed to play with the boys any longer. My life remained behind the walls of the House of the Princesses.

That's why I was surprised, one day, when word came from my father, the king, that my brother Amnon requested that I prepare some food for him. He said, "Go to your brother Amnon's house, and prepare food for him" (2 Sam 13:7). I'd heard he was sick, and I was worried about him. I dressed in one of my most beautiful robes and walked quickly through the palace corridors to his house. When I entered his room, he was lying in his bed. He asked me to prepare bread for him, and he wanted to see me prepare it with my own hands. I thought that was odd, but he always feared that someone would poison him. Maybe that's what he thought was the source of his illness.

I instructed the servants to bring me everything I needed to make the dough: flour, leaven, water. I mixed and kneaded the dough where he could see me, and then I placed the cakes in the fire to bake, but when they were ready, he would not eat them. He told everyone to leave the room, and then he said, "Bring the food into the chamber, so that I may eat from your hand" (2 Sam 13:10). I brought the cakes to my sweet brother with whom I had played games and run through the palace halls. I tenderly stroked his hair and wiped his brow with a cloth. I should have been more cautious.

Was it my fault? Suddenly he grabbed my hand and pulled me onto him. He said, "Come lie with me, my sister" (2 Sam 13:11). He told me he loved me, that he had loved me for years, not as a sister but as a lover. He said he was sick with love for me. I tried to pull away. I tried to scream for help, but he covered my mouth. I cried out in pain, and when he removed his hand I said:

> No, my brother, do not force me; for such a thing is not done in Israel; do not do anything so vile! As for me,

> where could I carry my shame? And as for you, you would be as one of the scoundrels in Israel. Now, therefore, I beg you, speak to the king; for he will not withhold me from you. (2 Sam 13:12–13)

But he would not listen. He pulled off my robe and pushed himself into me, and when he was finished, he pushed me away. "I hate you," he said. "I'll just send you away, you whore." And then he yelled at me, "Get out!" (2 Sam 13:15), but I replied, "No, my brother; for this wrong in sending me away is greater than the other that you did to me" (2 Sam 13:16).

He didn't love me; he didn't even want me. He called one of his servants into the room and told him, "Put this woman out of my presence and bolt the door after her" (2 Sam 13:17). The servant looked at me with pity, but he looked at his master with fear. He helped me put on my robe and then led me out into the darkness.

I stumbled down the dark hallways, lit only by occasional oil lamps, until I came upon a small altar. I scooped up a handful of ash from the altar and covered my head with the warm ashes. I tore my robe in an act of remorse for the loss of my virginity, for the loss of trust in my brother, for the loss of a future as a wife, for who would have me now? As I sat in front of the altar, I cried out to the God of Israel, Yahweh. I cried out for forgiveness—even though I didn't think I had done anything wrong.

Soon I heard footsteps coming down the hallway, and it was my brother Absalom. He saw me, disheveled with torn robe with ashes on my head, and he asked what had happened. I told him everything. As he held me in his arms, I sobbed. I could see in his eyes sincere pity for me and at the same time rage against his half-brother Amnon. He said, "Be quiet for now, my sister; he is your brother; do not take this to heart" (2 Sam 13:20). But he did. He took it to heart. He threatened to kill him in revenge, and I begged him not to.

The next day we requested to see our father, and we told him what his firstborn son had done. He was furious, but he said nothing to console me. Absalom presented him with the facts and with the laws that had been violated:

- Intercourse with a virgin (Exod 22:16–17)
- Laws of nakedness with female relationships (Exod 18:6)
- Adultery—resulting in death for both (Exod 20:18; Deut 22:22)
- Incestuous acts (Exod 18:22–24)
- Betrothed woman who is raped in the city vs. country (Deut 22:23)
- Nonbetrothed woman who is raped (Deut 22:28)

Finally, my father spoke. I knew at once that he would not punish Amnon. Instead, he said, "I cannot do anything, because he is my firstborn son." "What good is the law if it does not protect the innocent?" I asked. "What will become of me?" He didn't answer, he just turned and walked over to his balcony and looked out over his beautiful palace and the rooftops below. I left with Absalom and returned to his house where I remain today—a desolate woman. I never saw Amnon again.

Every day after that, Absalom looked on me with pity, and every day the rage grew in his heart. Two years to the day after I was raped, Absalom killed Amnon. It was sheepshearing time, and Absalom invited all the king's sons to come to his feast near Ephraim. When they were all drunk with wine, Absalom gave the word to his men to kill Amnon. The other sons of David ran back to Jerusalem, and when the king heard about the death of his firstborn son, he wept bitterly. I cannot say I mourned the death of my rapist, but I mourned the loss of my brother Absalom. You see Absalom had to escape the revenge of Amnon's murder. Will our father ever forgive him and allow him to return? He is all I have!

I have had many years to ponder these events. I can't help but think about my ancestor Tamar, for whom I was named. She was impregnated by her father-in-law, Judah. Tamar had twins, Perez and Zerah, whose unusual birth highlighted the importance of being a firstborn son. If being the firstborn son earns the father's favor, along with his inheritance, shouldn't it also carry some responsibility? Not for my brother Amnon. He taunted us with his firstborn status, thinking he was above the law, even the morals of a family.

I can't help but think about the look on my father's face when I told him that his son had raped me. I thought he looked guilty—that he hadn't protected me better, or that he had to choose between his daughter and his firstborn son. But much later, I learned another source of the look of guilt on his face.

I learned that another woman had joined our palace family, Bathsheba, and she was with child. I heard a terrible rumor about how she came to be the king's wife, and I couldn't believe my father could possibly do to her the same thing his despicable son did to me. He knows the law! He knows what our Yahweh requires of us! Could it be?

And where will this end? Absalom has killed Amnon. Sweet Chileab has died. Absalom is gone, rejected by our father. Adonijah is next in line. Will he become king? Or will another come along like Amnon and kill him? Is this the misery that the prophet, Samuel, promised would come with a monarchy? Why didn't we listen to him?

14
Jezebel

1 Kings 16—22

A Hebrew woman once told me there are three sides to every story: hers, mine, and God's. The Hebrews, as you may know, worship only one God. We Phoenicians have many gods to worship, so maybe my story has even more than three sides. But let me tell you mine.

I know you've heard of me. People say I'm evil, ruthless, heartless. Am I confident? Yes! Ambitious? Of course. Enjoy the power that comes with being queen? Yes, I do! Manipulative? Well, yes, we women have little choice if we are to have our way. Isn't that what it takes to be a powerful leader?

I am Jezebel, daughter of Ethbaal, king of Tyre. We are Sidonians, Phoenicians. I was a princess, and my marriage to Ahab, king of Samaria led to an alliance between Samaria (the Northern Kingdom, also known as Israel) and Tyre and Sidon on the coast of the great Mediterranean Sea. We knew we would be a powerful team. Ahab even agreed to allow me to claim the title "Priestess of Astarte," and although he pretended to be faithful to the Lord of Israel, he erected (for me, he said) an altar and temple to Baal in Samaria—a temple he built to please the people. Isn't that what a good leader does—that which pleases the people?

But I have come to despise everything about the people and

traditions of Israel. I despise their piety and ridiculous devotion to one god. I despise their prudish opinions about what our priests and priestesses do to please our gods. I despise their public prayers to their Lord God. I despise their priests, and I will continue to kill every one of them that I can. Every one! That disgusting Obadiah, my husband's palace steward, was a worshipper of Yahweh and had the gall to hide one hundred prophets of Yahweh from me, but I will find them. I will destroy them, and I will destroy Obadiah too.

Most of all I despise the one they call a prophet—Elijah, the Tishbite from Gilead. The scoundrel told Ahab there would be a three-year drought, and it happened! The drought led to a severe famine for the people of Samaria, and then Elijah returned and predicted the rains would come. Do we dare believe him? Was his prediction of drought just a hunch? A guess? Does he have some kind of magic power, or does he really speak for the Lord of the Israelites?

Elijah even challenged my husband, King Ahab, to a sacred duel on Mt. Carmel. Ahab told me all about it when he limped home in defeat. Ahab sent for 450 prophets to come to Mt. Carmel, and he challenged Elijah to see whose god was the true god. Our people went for the spectacle. Elijah told Ahab to bring two bulls, to carve them into pieces, and to build a tower of wood for a fire. Then Elijah said, "Then you call on the name of your god, and I will call on the name of the Lord; the god who answers by fire is indeed God" (1 Kgs 18:24). Ahab prepared his altar with wood and placed his bull on the altar. The Baal prophets said, "O Baal, answer us!" (1 Kgs 18:26). They danced, they shouted, they "cut themselves with swords and lances until the blood gushed out over them" (1 Kgs 18:28). They continued into the night, and nothing happened.

Elijah prepared his own altar just like Ahab's. But then he dug a trench around the altar and drenched the altar with water not once, not twice, but three times and said, "O Lord, God of Abraham, Isaac and Israel, let it be known today that you are God in Israel, that I am your servant, and that I have done all these things at your bidding. Answer me, O Lord, answer me, so this people will know that you, O Lord, are God, and that you have turned their hearts back" (1 Kgs 18:36–37).

How did he do it? His tower burned and the bull was consumed, despite being doused with water three times! Then the people claimed his Lord as their God, and Elijah commanded them to slaughter my prophets of Baal in the Kishon Valley. Ahab did nothing. He just returned to tell me what happened. But I will get revenge. Just wait!

I sent Elijah this message: "So may the gods do to me, and more also, if I do not make your life like the life of one of them by this time tomorrow" (1 Kgs 19:2). I heard that Elijah ran away, afraid. Good. He's no better a leader than Ahab—men who run away when they are afraid. Perhaps I am finally rid of that disgusting man who claims to be called by God. Then I heard Elijah anointed Elisha, another prophet, to succeed him. Must I endure another one like Elijah?

For years afterward, I thought we had succeeded in overcoming our enemies, but my king-husband made one bad decision after another. He grew weaker with every encounter. Ben-Hadad, king of Aram, laid siege to the city of Samaria and told Ahab he wanted his silver and gold, wives and children, and Ahab agreed! He agreed! He said, "As you say, my lord, O king, I am yours, and all that I have" (1 Kgs 20:4). What a weakling!

Fortunately, Ahab was inspired by someone—I know not who—to raise an army to pursue the king of Aram, and they caught that arrogant king while he was drinking with his officers. They destroyed the army, but the king fled. Year after year, Ben-Hadad and Ahab threatened to fight each other, but they never did. Finally, they established a treaty. What a weak leader he has become. He will do anything to save himself—even give up his children and wives—but not me. He knows he needs me. I am the true leader of our family, and he knows it.

And then there was the incident with Naboth's vineyard. Ahab sulked day after day about that vineyard, as if he didn't have enough land, gardens, farms, and vineyards himself. But he wanted Naboth's vineyard in Jezreel and mourned when Naboth refused to sell it to him. I finally said, "Why are you so depressed that you will not eat?... Do you now govern Israel? Get up, eat some food, and be cheerful; I will give you the vineyard of Naboth the Jezreelite" (1 Kgs 21:57).

I devised a plan and sent a note to some of our people: "Proclaim a fast, and seat Naboth at the head of the assembly; seat two scoundrels opposite him, and have them bring a charge against him, saying, 'You have cursed God and the king.' Then take him out and stone him to death" (1 Kgs 21:9–10).

They did just as I ordered them, and then word came back to me: "Naboth has been stoned; he is dead" (1 Kgs 21:14). Yes, I tricked Naboth and had him executed, and his remains were eaten by the dogs, but don't blame me alone. Do you not think the king was complicit? Of course he was. And that despicable Elijah predicted death for Ahab and the same fate as Naboth. How dare he insult the king of Samaria!

After that, Ahab became even weaker. He conspired with the kings of Judah, and he consulted with the new prophet Micaiah, but Ahab didn't like what Micaiah told him. As a final show of weakness, Ahab disguised himself as he went into battle—his last battle. A random arrow pierced his armor and, alas, the prophecy was fulfilled. Ahab was killed in battle against the king of Aram and was buried "by the pool of Samaria; the dogs licked up his blood, and the prostitutes washed themselves in it, according to the word of the Lord that he has spoken" (1 Kgs 22:38). How dare they treat the body of their leader in that way?

My only son, Ahaziah, succeeded his father, but only for two years. The holy, pious people of Israel called him evil, just like his parents, and predicted that his reign would be brief. He fell out of a window in the upper room and died from his injuries—but not without appealing to the god Baal-zebub to find out if he would die. But the despised Elijah—he seemed to appear out of nowhere—intercepted the messenger from Ahaziah and told him to return with the message that the king would indeed die.

And now he is dead, but even worse, he had no son when he died. A man named Joram succeeded him for twelve years—another of Ahab's sons—but not mine. They called him evil, too, and I would agree. He removed the shrines of Baal—the ones my husband built for me to worship Baal and Astarte! Some said he was a better leader than Ahab. What is the measure of a true leader? One who bows to the superstitions and old ways of a people who are destined to be destroyed?

I cannot seem to get away from these so-called men of God. Elijah has finally disappeared. His naïve followers said he was taken up to the heavens in a whirlwind; others said he was taken up in a chariot of fire. These delusional people will believe anything. His successor, Elisha, anointed Jehu king of Israel—Jehu, the army commander—even as Joram was still king! He told him to conquer Joram and destroy the house of Ahab, and said, "The dogs shall eat Jezebel in the territory of Jezreel, and no one shall bury her" (2 Kgs 9:10). Should I be worried, after all these years? For twelve years I have endured this son of Ahab who was called evil, but better than his brother, my son, and his father, my husband. Must I now endure his successor, the commander turned king?

I just heard Jehu killed Joram and desecrated his body by throwing it "on the plot of ground belonging to Naboth the Jezreelite" (2 Kgs 9:25). He mocks me, and now Jehu is moving on to Jezreel. Maybe this is finally the end for me, but I will not go quietly. I will go like the whore that they think I am—just because I don't worship the way they do. Just watch me. After I die, how will I be remembered? As a strong queen or vile heretic? I suppose it depends on who tells the story. But know this: I am proud. I am a leader. Just watch me.

First, I lined my eyes with dark black ink, then I arranged my hair in coils. Now I'm looking out of a window in the upper tower of the palace, and there he is. I see him. The mighty, murderous Jehu. There he is, entering the gate, and I shout out to him, "Is it peace, Zimri, murderer of your master?" (2 Kgs 9:31) Oh, he looks so smug. Do you know what he is doing? He is ordering my two eunuchs to throw me down. Will I fall from a window like my son? Fall to my death at the hands of those who are sworn to protect me? No! I am Jezebel, wife of Ahab, mother of Ahaziah, queen of Samaria, priestess of Astarte. Take your hands off me, you traitors. I am Jezebel!

15
Huldah

2 Kings 22—25; 2 Chronicles 34

I've been telling them for years. God has spoken to me, and it is an angry voice I hear. But they forget. They turn their backs on God. They worship the gods of the Canaanites in the Lord's sacred temple in Jerusalem. Have they forgotten that our God, Yahweh, delivered us from bondage in Egypt? From wandering in the desert for forty years? From the Canaanites, the Amorites, the Ammonites, the Hittites, the Jebusites, and the Philistines? Deliver us now, O God, from our ignorance.

I've been telling them. I mutter the words softly while praying in the outer court of the temple, and I shout them as I walk around the temple walls that separate the temple grounds from the Second Quarter where I, Huldah, live. Day after day I come to the temple to hear the words of the Lord, but even the priests do not read or speak them. They say one of the Books of the Law has been misplaced, but how can that be? Is it possible our ungodly kings destroyed the scrolls, for fear the people would hear the Word of the Lord? What became of the tablets in the Ark of the Covenant—the holy ark that the priests still carry about on their shoulders? Moses told us to write on our doorposts and our gates: "Hear O Israel: The Lord is our God, the Lord alone" (Deut 6:4). The Lord *alone.* But the people don't remember.

How long, O Lord, must we see one king after another turn his back on you? Even our beloved King David, though great in many ways, was far from righteous. But many have been much, much worse. My parents told me of Manasseh, son of Hezekiah, who encouraged his people to worship the Baals. He sacrificed his own son to the Baals. What kind of king does that? What kind of father does that? Oh, he repented, but he had already instilled this evil in his son Amon, who was assassinated by his own people after only two years of his reign.

I often wonder about the conversations and conspiracies that go on in the king's palace. So many people want to be next to rule. We are told that God has chosen our kings, from the time of our first king, Saul, when the prophet Samuel anointed him king on behalf of God. Does God still choose our kings? Did God choose the little boy, Josiah, to succeed his father—at only eight years of age? People have questioned God about this, but I think God did, and I think God surrounded little Josiah with people who taught him well: Zephaniah, Jeremiah, and me—Huldah. Yes, God calls women to lead, to serve, and to prophesy, just as God calls men.

Josiah was a special child, and as he grew to be a young man, "He did what was right in the sight of the Lord, and walked in the ways of his ancestor David" (2 Chr 34:2). I am a few years older than Josiah, so I have watched him grow. When he was twenty-six years old, his true leadership began. He sought to rid the land of the idols and shrines that had been built for the people to worship other gods—a violation of the very first two commandments given to Moses: "You shall have no other gods before me" and "You shall not make for yourself an idol....You shall not bow down to them or worship them; for I the Lord your God am a jealous God" (Exod 20:3–5). I would see Josiah as he came to the temple each day for prayer. He acknowledged me. He *saw* me. He *heard* my words of warning.

One day he greeted me, and as he turned to walk away, I followed behind him. I said to him from behind, quietly so only he could hear me, "Good King Josiah, enter the house of the Lord and *see* it. See how the people have allowed it to fall into disrepair. See the disrespect, the dismissal, the disarray represented there—even by the priests, and do something about it. Restore it for God's worship. Restore us as God's people." I said the words softly, so as not to draw the attention of temple leaders standing around, so they would think it was just odd Huldah, mumbling her daily prayers and prophecies.

This happened many years ago, but I remember it well. He slowly turned to acknowledge the voice behind him, or perhaps to chastise the woman who spoke so boldly to the king, but I quickly slipped away behind an open door. He saw only strangers and merchants and a few worshippers going about their business, and so he went on his way to the temple.

Some days later when I returned to the temple grounds, I heard the sounds of workers in the temple and saw them carrying baskets laden with rubble out of the temple. They were cleaning out the temple! I saw Shaphan, the king's secretary, overseeing the work, and I knew King Josiah had heard me! Shaphan was outside the temple talking to the high priest, Hilkiah. They were arguing about something, so I went closer to hear their argument. The high priest was objecting to the workers in the temple being unsupervised by him and the other priests. He said they would probably steal all the money that has been given to the temple—money that I'm sure benefited him. But Shaphan told him the orders came from the king:

> Let [the money] be given into the hand of the workers who have the oversight of the house of the Lord; let them give it to the workers who are at the house of the Lord, repairing the house, that is, to the carpenters, to the builders, to the masons; and let them use it to buy timber and quarried stone to repair the house. But no accounting shall be asked from them for the money that is delivered into their hand, for they deal honestly. (2 Kgs 22:5–7)

What a wise, young king to trust the workers more than the priests. I had wondered for many years where our money was going, for truly it was not going for the upkeep of the temple. I watched as the high priest, Hilkiah, sulked as he entered the temple.

Moments later, there were loud, excited voices at the entrance of the temple, and the workers came running to Shaphan with news of a discovery. Out of the temple emerged Hilkiah, carrying a package, but he did not look as excited as the workers. The package was covered in dust, but it looked like the scrolls I'm told the priests used to read, especially on the holy days and the Sabbath. Could it be? I quickly returned to my home in the Second Quarter of Jerusalem and sat in prayer, awaiting God's guidance for what might happen next. "Speak to me, O God," I prayed. "Speak through me, that your people will know your will." And then I waited.

Soon after, many men knocked on my door. My husband Shallum brought them in: Hilkiah, the high priest; Akbor, one of King Josiah's officials; Shaphan, the royal secretary and his son Ahikam; and Asaiah, the king's attendant. I am known as a prophetess, and many people—men and women—have sought my advice, but I don't think I have ever been visited by so many powerful men at one time.

Shaphan spread the scroll before me and told me it had been found in the temple during cleaning, and the king wanted to verify its authenticity. The king wanted *me* to verify its authenticity. He specifically asked for Huldah, the prophetess, who lives in the Second Quarter! Shaphan told me that the king was in great distress to learn of the scroll, such distress that he tore his garments as a sign of grief; he feared that these words, possibly the words of Moses himself, had been forgotten, at best, or hidden, at worst.

I read the words on the scroll that Shaphan presented to me, and I shuddered when I saw what struck fear and grief in our young king. This is the Word of God for the people of God, but we have not been observing the laws written on the scroll; therefore, we would certainly suffer the consequences. This was the scroll of the Covenant, and we have not honored it. The consequences would surely mean destruction for us. And then I spoke; or rather, God spoke through me:

> Thus says the Lord, the God of Israel: Tell the man who sent you to me, Thus says the Lord, I will indeed bring disaster on this place and on its inhabitants—all the words of the book that the king of Judah has read. Because they have abandoned me and have made offerings to other gods, so that they have provoked me to anger with all the work of

> their hands, therefore my wrath will be kindled against this place, and it will not be quenched. But as to the king of Judah, who sent you to inquire of the Lord, thus shall you say to him, Thus says the Lord, the God of Israel: Regarding the words that you have heard; because your heart was penitent, and you humbled yourself before the Lord, when you heard how I spoke against this place, and against its inhabitants, that they should become a desolation and a curse, and because you have torn your clothes and wept before me, I also have heard you, says the Lord. Therefore, I will gather you to your ancestors, and you shall be gathered to your grave in peace; your eyes shall not see all the disaster that I will bring on this place. (2 Kgs 22:15–20)

I wish you had been there, to see the terror in the eyes of those who were present. To sense their fear as they returned to the king to confirm his worst imaginings. The king called all the people to the house of the Lord, and he read the entire book of the covenant to us. He read it himself! And then he "made a covenant before the Lord, to follow the Lord, keeping his commandments, his decrees, and his statutes, with all his heart and all his soul" (2 Kgs 23:3).

We promised too! All the people promised! And then, right before our eyes, the king ordered the priests to bring out of the temple all the vessels and images that had been used to worship Baal and his consort, Asherah. He burned them and crushed them to ashes. He deposed the idolatrous priests and tore down their houses and high altars, pillars and sacred poles.

Then King Josiah commanded us to observe the Passover festival that had been ignored since the days of the judges—yet another sign of how far we had strayed from our covenant with Yahweh. Oh, it was a Passover to remember! We celebrated the Feast of Unleavened Bread and remembered how God brought the Israelites out of slavery in Egypt. The king, himself, provided Passover lambs for all of us, and we wept as the lambs were sacrificed for us. Over and over, we promised God that we would never again forget our many blessings or forget who God called us to be.

But we did, and my great misfortune was that I have lived to be an old woman and have seen fulfilled the very words spoken from my mouth. Our good king Josiah died in battle and was mourned a hero after a reign of thirty-one years. It has now been a little more than twenty years since King Josiah died. Oh, how far we have fallen.

After King Josiah's death, we had one evil, weak king after another, and we soon became pawns of Egypt and later of Babylon. The Babylonian king, Nebuchadnezzar, lay siege to Jerusalem, eventually taking the king to Babylon as a prisoner, along with thousands of royal persons, officials, priests, soldiers, artisans, and even treasures from the house of the Lord.

King Nebuchadnezzar appointed a king in Jerusalem, but he rebelled against Nebuchadnezzar, and that was the last straw. We heard Nebuchadnezzar coming, his great armies causing the ground to tremble as they surrounded our city. For months we were under siege, and there was no food for our people. And what did our king do? He fled one night through a breach in the city wall, along with his sons and his soldiers. Escaped while his people starved. But he didn't get far before he and all his men were caught. The king of Babylon "slaughtered [all of his sons] before his eyes, then put out [his] eyes; they bound him in fetters and took him to Babylon" (2 Kgs 25:7).

Now Nebuchadnezzar's armies are destroying our great city, destroying the walls that have protected us, destroying the house of the Lord, the great temple in Jerusalem, carrying away the vessels, the bronze and silver and gold, the pomegranate carvings on the pillars. Anyone left behind in the city is being carried off to exile in Babylon. And, oh God, now I see the fire.

The house of the Lord is consumed in flames, the king's house too, and the fire is spreading to the Second Quarter. My beloved temple. My beloved city. My beloved people. All destroyed. The streets are filling with thick smoke, and it seeps through my open windows. I struggle to breathe. I gasp for breath. I am old and cannot run.

I fall to my knees and pray, "Hear O Israel: The Lord is our God. The Lord alone."

16
Esther

Old Testament Book of Esther; Apocryphal Book of Esther

Do you know anyone who will celebrate a birthday soon? What do you do to celebrate your birth? Have you ever felt sad on your birthday? I must confess that I have often felt melancholy on my birthday—that is, until this last one, when I finally realized why I was born.

My name is Hadassah, but you may know me better by the name I was given in Persia: Esther. Maybe I sensed sadness all around me even as a baby. You see, I was born far, far away from my homeland of Judea. I was born in Susa, in the land of Persia. Before my birth, our family had lived for several generations with other Jews whose families were carried off to Babylonia, later called Persia, when the invading Babylonians destroyed our beautiful city of Jerusalem and our sacred temple. I can't remember my father at all. He died when I was a small child, and my mother died when I was only eight years old. I only faintly recall my mother's beautiful but sad face as she sang the weekly Shabbat prayer. Each night, as she would rock me to sleep, she would sing:

Hadassah, Hadassah,
Bright, shining star.

Always remember
Who you are.

My cousin Mordecai raised me from childhood and taught me the faith of my mother and my father—faith in the God of the Hebrews. He told me stories of our people and our God whose name was Yahweh...Adonai...El Shaddai. Cousin Mordecai is wonderful, and though he has tried to give me a happy life, it seems that every birthday is a sad reminder of something lost: mother, father, homeland, freedom.

You see, the Persians do not share our faith in Yahweh. Some have allowed us to worship in the ways of our ancestors, but others treat us with ridicule at best, persecution at worst. I learned as a young woman that persecution comes in many forms: religious, ethnic, social, and even gender persecution. In fact, I became a queen many years ago because of the persecution of another woman. May I tell you the story?

The King of Persia, King Ahasuerus, ruled over a vast empire: 127 provinces from India to Ethiopia! He was known for his elaborate parties, but in the third year of his reign in Susa—the winter palace near Babylon—the party lasted 180 days! Military leaders, governors, and royalty came and went for six months! The party culminated in two seven-day banquets, one given by King Ahasuerus to the men and one given by Queen Vashti to the women. No expense was spared in preparations for the banquets; food and wine—and more wine—were consumed in great quantities.

I heard stories from the women who served the king and his guests, stories of how the men became increasingly drunk with wine as the days went on. And the more they drank, the more familiar they became with the women who served them.

On the seventh day of the banquet, the king sent for Queen Vashti to come dance before his guests. I heard he commanded her to come "wearing her crown," and some people understood his commandment to mean for her to wear *only her crown.* When word went out all over Susa, from the partygoers to the exiles, that she had refused the king's command, we were shocked and frightened at the possible result of the king's anger. No woman refused her husband's orders—especially if her husband was the king. But Vashti did.

The king was enraged. He consulted his sages who predicted that if the king did not make an example of Vashti, all the other women in the kingdom would refuse their husbands' orders as well. Ha! Did they think the world would stop spinning if women were considered equal partners in a relationship, worthy of consulting, not only of taking their husbands' orders? I say, "Good for you, Vashti!"

We never found out what happened to Vashti. We know she was banished from the king's presence, but we never heard of her again.

Without a queen now, Ahasuerus held a contest to find a new queen. I guess you would call it a beauty contest. The most beautiful young women in Persia were taken from their homes, and the king's eunuchs spent a full year making them even more beautiful with cosmetic treatments. At the end of the year, the king would choose the most beautiful woman in the group to be queen. I know this, because I was one of those women.

You might think I would be happy to live in the palace for a year, but I was not. When I was selected for the king's beauty contest, I became a captive. I dared not reveal my ethnic and religious identity, because I had no idea how I would be treated if they knew I was a Jew. I feared for those who knew me as well, like my cousin, Mordecai. But my situation was not unlike that of my Hebrew brothers and sisters in captivity in Persia. I could whine, lament, even give up, or I could make the best of my situation, praising God in my words and deeds, quietly keeping the traditions of my faith and boldly keeping strong in my faith. I chose the latter, and even though the eunuchs never knew whom I was worshipping, they admired me and even favored me with special attention.

The one thing that sustained me during that lonely year, besides my faith in God, was the daily message I received from my cousin, Mordecai. Somehow—I'll never know how he did it—he smuggled messages to me. Often the messages would contain words from the Torah, the sacred text of our people. The words comforted me, but I was not happy. I could not wait to hear whom the king had chosen. I was ready to go home! But guess what happened next? I was chosen queen. Me, Queen Esther! And dear, sweet Mordecai continued to come to the palace gate every day with a message of comfort and encouragement.

The next chain of events was hard for me to understand. I was not privy to political maneuvers and never will understand all the factions that make up the kingdom, so I will explain it the best I can. You see, one day when Mordecai was outside the gate trying to hear news about the beauty contest, he overheard two of the king's eunuchs plotting to kill the king. Mordecai sent word to me about what he heard. Even at the risk of personal harm, I could not allow this to happen if I could prevent it, so I sent word of the plot to the king. The traitors were hanged on gallows.

I was so naïve. I thought Mordecai might be rewarded for his deeds, but the king seemed to forget all about it—even though the deed had been duly recorded. And Mordecai's life became worse instead of better. A hateful man named Haman was promoted above all the officials. He was so arrogant that he made everyone bow down before him. But Mordecai would not. He refused to bow before anyone but God! Haman was furious, and when he learned that Mordecai was a Jew, he vowed to destroy all the Jews. He even misled the king about the Jews, and without ever really mentioning them by name, he persuaded the king to agree to their destruction. He cast lots, we called them *pur*, to determine when the destruction would take place, and the lot fell on the thirteenth day of the twelfth month, Adar.

The decree went out from the king. Poor Mordecai. I learned that he was walking through the city clothed in sackcloth and ashes, wailing at the gate of the king. I was devastated, too, when I heard the news. Mordecai begged me to go to the king on behalf of our people, but what could I do? Going before the king without his invitation could carry the penalty of death! But how selfish of me; what was I thinking? All of my people were facing death. Would I be silent if I could make a difference? At least I had the favor of the king.

I'll never forget Mordecai's words: "[Esther] perhaps you have come to royal dignity for just such a time as this" (Esth 4:14).

I returned to my room and prayed the entire night. Was God

asking me to risk my life for my people? I prayed for courage and guidance. The next day, I asked Mordecai to have all faithful Jews fast for three days, and my maids, with whom I shared my faith, joined me in my fast. On the third day, I summoned my nerve and approached the king. How happy I was when he extended his golden scepter to me, a sign that I could enter his presence. He asked me what I wanted, but I could not just blurt out my request, so I invited him—and Haman—to join me for supper.

When he came for supper, he asked what I wanted. It was obvious that he adored me; he offered me half his kingdom, though I admit he was drunk when he did. I still could not summon the courage to talk to him about Haman's plans to kill the Jews, so I invited them to dinner the next day. What a coward I was!

In the meantime, Haman went around bragging, "I dined with King Ahasuerus and Queen Esther." He grew more and more arrogant, and Mordecai's refusal to bow to him incensed him all the more. He decided, on his own, to build gallows on which to hang Mordecai. As it happened, that very night, the king was reading the royal records—his favorite treatment for insomnia—and he came across Mordecai's favor to him, which saved Mordecai's life. He learned that Mordecai had not been rewarded for his deeds, and the next morning he ordered Haman to robe Mordecai and parade him through the square. Imagine Haman's disgust; at the very moment he planned to go into the king's presence to get permission to kill Mordecai, he had to honor him for his loyalty to the king.

Was the king's discovery an accident, or was the hand of God guiding him? That night the king and Haman came once more to my chambers for a banquet. Finally, I drew up the courage to reveal to the king my true identity and tell him of the plot to kill my people, the Jews. When the king heard of the plot, he turned to me and said, "Who is he, and where is he, who has presumed to do this?" (Esth 7:5) I pointed to Haman and said, "A foe and enemy, this wicked Haman!" (Esth 7:6). The wicked weasel begged me for his life, but to no avail; King Ahasuerus commanded that Haman be hung on the same gallows he built to hang my cousin.

The king gave me Haman's house and gave Mordecai his signet ring. He sent out messengers reversing the decree to kill the Jews.

He even gave the Jews permission to defend themselves if any soldiers tried to harm them. And the most surprising part of all is that he gave the Jews one day to plunder the goods of Persians. What a celebration we had! We should not have enjoyed the revenge, but we did. We even heard of Persians professing to be Jews for their own protection and wellbeing. What is the world coming to?

The king continued to hold me in his favor, and Mordecai became second to the king in power. Our people have never forgotten how God saved them through a faithful, courageous woman. Every year we celebrate Purim on the fourteenth and fifteenth days of the twelfth month of Adar. The name of our festival reminds us of the lots, *pur*, that Haman cast. What was to be for our destruction led to our salvation.

From now on, I will make a special prayer on my birthday, because I finally realized why I was born. God needed me to do something important and then made sure I was surrounded by people who would prepare me to be strong and faithful. God is, indeed, an awesome God!

17
The Innkeeper

Matthew 1; Luke 1—2

Oppressed! Oppressive! Oppression! Those are the words that describe my life, my very existence. And not just me, but everyone I know. Especially those of us in Bethlehem, in Judea, right now.

We live in a dangerous time and place. There is even talk of revolution against the Romans. Still, the emperor threatens us with every new decree. What new oppression will come next? More taxes, to be sure, and he'll probably decree that we must pay them using his coins, bearing his image. Will he also make us worship him as the god he thinks he is? Not I. Never! I touch the doorpost of the inn as I enter and speak the words taught to me as a child: "Hear O Israel: The Lord is our God. The Lord is One."

To make sure any of us who own property pay the proper tax, Augustus has decreed that we must all be registered through a census. He put Quirinius, Governor of Syria, in charge. And to make it even more inconvenient, he said Judeans must travel to their ancestral place of birth to be counted. What's the point of that?

Can you imagine how many people have been packing themselves into Bethlehem, the City of David, over the past few weeks? King David, with his seven wives (and that's only the ones whose sons he counted) and many children—just imagine how many offspring there are today. Don't forget that his son and successor, Solomon, had seven hundred wives who were princesses and three hundred concubines. Plus, it's been almost one thousand years since King David died, and that's a LOT of offspring. I feel like half of them are packed into my inn right now! Families who live in Bethlehem are welcoming as many relatives as they can—such is our tradition of hospitality—and every inn I know is full of people who have no family in Bethlehem. The multitude of humans walking through the city, standing in lines waiting for bread, breathing the air that seems to be as scarce as a place to sleep, makes everything so oppressive.

Normally I love my town of Bethlehem, and I love my job as an innkeeper. I'm proud that I have been able to keep this property and this business after the death of my husband—in spite of the hateful things people say about me, a widow, allowing strange men to sleep under my roof. Normally I love welcoming strangers, hearing about their journeys, learning about other lands and people. But this census makes everything just so oppressive.

And I am also very tired. I have been preparing meals and cleaning rooms for days with no rest. Strangers pound on the door to the inn at all hours of the day and night, begging for a place to stay, shouting insults at me when I tell them we have no room. But we have no room!

And then, one night a few weeks ago as I was cleaning the last of the tables from dinner, I heard a quiet tap on the door. I walked to the door, opened it, and there before me was yet another couple, weary from a long journey. The man appeared to be older than the woman, but who knows; he was so dusty and looked so weary. He held her arm gently as if she was having trouble standing. And then I noticed why. "She is going to have a baby!" (I think I said it out loud.) Maybe soon. Maybe real soon.

He tells me they have traveled all the way from Nazareth in Galilee, and this is his destination, because he is from the family of David. He tells me that everyone he talked to told him there was nowhere to stay in Bethlehem, that he may as well sleep outside the city walls, or maybe journey over to Bethany to try to find a place to stay there. But it was late, he said, and his wife was beginning to have the pains of childbirth.

I don't know why this couple touched my heart. Just when I was going to say AGAIN "We have no room," I looked over their shoulders into the night sky, and it looked like the twinkling stars in the heavens had just gotten brighter. I heard something, like the jingling of thousands of tiny bells. I remembered my mother who told me stories of Abraham and Sarah and the angels who visited them. She said, "You never know when you might be entertaining angels." "But, Mother" (I said to my long-dead mother), "we have no room!"

About that time, the breeze shifted, and I caught the smell of the stable where we keep our animals: one cow, two sheep, one donkey, and several chickens. It's not really a pleasant smell. Well, the hay smells good, but when I have to go and gather up their—you know what—it doesn't smell so good. But it gave me an idea. I told the young couple (his name was Joseph and hers was Mary) that I would try to make them a comfortable place to rest for the night, but they'd have to share it with the animals. You'd have thought I offered them a room in the king's palace!

I took a blanket, a bucket of water, and a loaf of bread with me, and I led them to the stable. I fluffed up some hay for a bed; Joseph helped Mary lie down. Before I told him good night, she was already asleep. She must have been exhausted from her long journey. Even her donkey looked exhausted!

I was too. I went straight to bed and fell fast asleep. I was dreaming of all the people who had pounded on the door to the inn all day: BAM, BAM, BAM! I couldn't even get away from it in my sleep! And then I realized I wasn't dreaming. Good grief, I thought. Can't they read the sign that says we have no room? Then I realized the pounding on the door was accompanied by a voice that cried with panic, "Help!" I opened the door, and there stood Joseph with a look of terror on his face. "It's Mary," he said, "and the baby is coming."

I've never had a baby myself, but I've seen a lot of babies born, and I've assisted many midwives over the years, so I gathered up what I knew I would need: hot water, a knife, twine, some cloths. I hurried out to the stable and shooed the animals away. Then I went to Mary to see how she was doing. She was so young, and she looked just as terrified as Joseph was. I told them not to be afraid, everything would be just fine—and I prayed that it would.

Joseph tried to distract his worried wife in between the pains by talking to her in a soothing voice. I was paying attention to the pains, trying to give them some privacy in their conversation, but I overheard some of what they said.

Joseph was telling her about a dream he had, where an angel told him that Mary would have a son, and he should be named Jesus. Mary told him about seeing and hearing an angel who told her she would have a son, and he should be named Jesus. She said the angel told her he would be known as the Son of God! They reminded each other of this in a familiar way, as if they had told each other the same stories over and over for nine months. I could tell they earnestly believed this was from God.

Childbirth makes people say weird things. Especially the mother. But they seemed certain of what they were saying.

And then he arrived. And it was a *he,* just like they said—or just like they said the angel said—a little baby boy that they named right then and there: Jesus. Oh, they probably officially named him after eight days when they found a rabbi to conduct the obligatory circumcision ritual and again after forty days when they took him to the temple for Mary's purification. But they already called him Jesus—from the moment he took his first breaths. That's a heavy name to place on a baby. It means "The Lord's Salvation." And then I remembered that Joseph told Mary that the angel in his dream said their son would save his people from their sins.

So, I wrap the baby in swaddling cloths, and place him in the only crib available, the manger where we put food for the animals. I tell his mother to get some rest, and as if things could not get any stranger, there appeared at the door of the stable a couple of grungy shepherds with their sheep and a barking sheepdog. The shepherds glowed—really, they glowed—as if they had just seen the Lord God! They said, "We have come to see the child that the angels told us about, a Savior, the Messiah. We were told he would be wrapped in cloths and lying in a manger" (paraphrased from Luke 2:11–12). When their eyes got accustomed to the dark stable, lit only by a small lantern, they saw the happy father, the weary mother, and their newborn son lying in the manger, and they just cried like babies. They fell on their knees and prayed aloud to God, prayers of joy and thanksgiving. They kept saying, "Glory to God in the highest heaven" and "Peace on earth" (Luke 2:14). I was stunned. Shocked. But sweet Mary just smiled, as though she were treasuring this moment in her heart...a treasure forever.

After they were registered, and after their temple obligations were complete, Mary and Joseph and Jesus left Bethlehem and returned to Nazareth. I will not likely live long enough to see this Jesus grow into a man, but I pray for him every night. I pray for his mother and father too. I pray that their visions and dreams will come true, that their son will save us from our sins. Oh yes, we are sinful people! The burden of our sinfulness is as oppressive as the burden of Roman rule. But I have hope. I have seen the face of Jesus. I have seen the face of salvation. I have seen the face of God.

Just think of it: God came to us! *To us!* God came to us in the form of a baby named Jesus. I saw him right there, lying in a manger. And who should be his first visitors (other than me, of course) but some hardworking, smelly shepherds. That must mean that God loves *all* of us, came for *all* of us. Even me. Hallelujah! Glory to God in the highest heaven! Amen.

18
The Shepherd

Luke 2

I have one of the most wonderful jobs a woman could have! I get to spend my days—and sometimes my nights—in God's beautiful creation, strolling over these hills of Judea, tending a flock of sheep. No, really! I'm very grateful for this work. After all, there aren't many things a woman can do for money—at least not many honorable things. I'm not good with my hands, so forget weaving or sewing or making pottery. But I'm really good with animals, especially sheep. I know each one by name, all one hundred of them, and they know my voice when I call them.

Like this little rascal—well, that's her name, Rascal. I've had to rescue her a few times. That's what a good shepherd does. One time she got away, and I feared the wolves would get her, so I had to leave the other ninety-nine with my faithful sheepdog guarding them to go and rescue her. Here's my sheepdog; her name is Esther, which is Hebrew for Star, but I call her Stella. Say hello, Stella!

Esther is one of my heroines, because she saved our people, Israel, when they were in exile in Persia. We read her story every year during the feast of Purim. I love that story, love to hear how God saves our people—stubborn as we are—over and over, and how Esther helps. But I really love the Psalms—especially where they sing about shepherds—about God as the Good Shepherd. I sing them when I'm afraid out here in the dark night. One says, "Give ear, O Shepherd of Israel, you who lead Joseph like a flock!" (Ps 80:1). Here's my favorite: "The Lord is my shepherd. I shall not want. He makes me lie down in green pastures; he leads me beside still waters; he restores my soul" (Ps 23:1–2).

That's the kind of shepherd God is to me. That's the kind of shepherd I want to be.

Oh, but there's something I want to tell you! You won't believe what happened tonight! Usually it's pretty boring out here—with the occasional bandit or wild animal to deal with. Boring can be good—especially during times like this when the emperor calls for a census and there are so many people in town that it's hard to walk through the streets. The inns are full of people who have come to Bethlehem, the City of David, because they are descendants of the House of David—our great King David.

But let me tell you what happened tonight—it was anything but boring! I still don't know what it means, but something very special happened to me tonight. I think I saw the face of God.

Earlier tonight, as the stars popped out one by one in the night sky, suddenly a group of stars came together in a cluster, pulsating like a living, glowing creature in the sky. I saw it first and shouted to the other shepherds who were working with me. They came running from the other side of the hill to see what I was looking at, and we all just stood there, amazed and afraid. Now, don't think I'm strange when I tell you what happened next. We heard a voice coming from the cluster of light that said, "Do not be afraid; for see—I am bringing you good news of great joy for all the people: to you is born this day in the city of David a Savior, who is the Messiah, the Lord. This will be a sign for you: you will find a child wrapped in bands of cloth and lying in a manger" (Luke 2:10–12).

A savior? The Messiah? The Lord? We've been waiting so long for the Messiah to come, and Isaiah said there would be signs, but the voice said it was a baby. A newborn baby lying in a manger.

And the voice said, "Do not be afraid." How can we not be afraid? We're hearing voices! And then to make matters worse, suddenly bursts of light appeared in the sky. It looked and sounded like a glowing choir of angels. And we heard them say in unison, "Glory to God in the highest heaven, and on earth peace among those whom he favors" (Luke 2:14). And then they were gone. Poof! Just like that, gone into the heavens.

"What had just happened?" we asked each other. Did everyone hear the angels, even the crowds in Bethlehem, or was their message just for us? Why would a heavenly choir announce the birth of the Messiah to us? We're just hardworking, illiterate shepherds. But we heard the message, and right over the hills was Bethlehem. The angels said the Messiah was somewhere in that town full of residents and pilgrims. A baby lying in a manger?

I said, "Let us go now to Bethlehem and see this thing that has taken place, which the Lord has made known to us" (Luke 2:15). The other shepherds looked at me like I was a crazy woman. Just abandon our flocks? We could lose our jobs! But not old Reuben. He was the one who would always lead us in prayer when we were afraid. Many times, he had told us about the Messiah. He said he would go with me, so we went, leaving the other shepherds in the field watching our flock. All but Rascal, she went with me. Stella insisted on going with me too, and I'm glad she did.

Reuben and I walked over the hills to Bethlehem. It was almost midnight, and the city doors were locked, so we knocked on the little door beside the big gates. The night watchman let us in, and then we just stood there, not knowing where to go. But Stella tossed her head to the right and barked as if to say, "Go this way." There was a lantern hanging in the opening of a little cave molded into the city wall beside an inn whose door was locked tight. I guess they had no more room. We walked a little closer, and I heard a cow "moo," and a donkey "hee-haw." My little Rascal "baaaaaed" in response.

We peeked our heads into the cave's opening, and there in a manger filled with straw was a newborn baby—wrapped in the cloths that mothers use to swaddle their babies. A woman was there tending the mother—a midwife, I supposed, or maybe someone from the inn. The father stood over him like a guard, and the mother knelt beside him, stroking his little head and cooing a song. She saw us and nodded for us to come in. She looked so tired but happy, and I saw something else in her eyes. She looked...worried. I wondered why a mother would possibly worry when she had a beautiful, healthy newborn baby. But she looked worried, as if she could see his entire life unfolding before her eyes, and she was worried about all that could happen to him. Mothers are like that, aren't they?

We sat down beside the manger and told the mother our story, of the bright light, and the angels, and the message. The midwife looked astonished, but the mother—her name was Mary—and the father—his name was Joseph—they didn't think we were crazy at all. She had seen an angel, and he had a dream about an angel, and they received the same message: Name the child Jesus—"God saves."

Mary asked me if I wanted to hold her baby, and I took him into my arms and rocked him. I looked into his little face, and...Have you ever looked at someone and thought you were looking into the face of God? I don't think I have. But tonight, in Bethlehem, I thought I was looking into the face of God. Now don't get me wrong. All babies are special, but I've looked at many babies and haven't thought I was looking at God. But something happened to me tonight. When his little fingers wrapped around mine, I felt like I had been touched by God.

Reuben and I went back to the shepherds and told them everything that happened. Everyone was amazed when they heard our stories, and miraculously, they didn't think we were crazy! After all, we'd all heard the angels that night! We all told anyone who would listen, "To you...and you...and you...to all of you is born this day in the city of David a Savior, who is the Messiah, the Lord" (Luke 2:11).

I will remember this night—this holy night—for as long as I live. Thanks be to God!

19
Mary, Mother of Jesus

Matthew 1—4; Luke 1—2; 23; John 19

God, how I hate this place. It reeks of sorrow, of suffering, of death. Here I have stood for hours, and now the sky is turning dark, the clouds gather, a storm is coming, and then it will be a dark place of the dead, like Sheol. Where are you, God? I am trying, God, but I cannot feel your presence. My body is so heavy with grief. They call this place Golgotha, the Place of the Skull. For me it will always be the place where my only son died.

My name is Mary. For many years I was known as the young wife of Joseph. People taunted him for taking such a young girl to be his wife, old widower that he was. But now I am known as the widow of Joseph of Nazareth. Three decades ago, I became known as the mother of Jesus, but until recently, he was away from Nazareth, so I was known as mother and grandmother of the sons and daughters of Joseph from his first wife. Jesus was my only child, my son, my little lamb. As much as I have loved him these thirty years and more—and never more than today—I have tried to prevent this day from coming, even from the moment he was conceived in my womb.

I was only a child when I came under the protection of kind Joseph of Nazareth. He was a builder—often away on the emperor's building projects, and he promised to take me as his wife when I became a woman. During one of his absences, I awoke one morning feeling sick. I described my feeling to one of the women who served Joseph, and she told me I must be with child. How could that be? I had never known a man. All day I sat by the well under the shade of a tree and prayed to God, "Please God, do not let this child grow in me. It will be a tragedy for me, for my family, and for my child." Tragedy indeed! The Law would allow my betrothed to take me before the elders to be convicted of adultery, probably to be stoned to death.

Late in the afternoon, as I grew faint from not eating or drinking, I began to feel around me a presence of bright light, and in my head, I heard a voice. My heart told me it was the voice of an angel. I didn't understand the words, but I remembered them: Jesus, Son of the Most High, David, Jacob, Holy Spirit, Son of God, Elizabeth. None of it made sense to me except the last one: Elizabeth.

And so, I hurried to the hill country, to the home of my kinswoman, Elizabeth, and her husband, the priest Zechariah. She, too, was with child—the first for her. At her advanced age, everyone had thought she was barren. When she embraced me, I could feel her little one kicking his feet, and she uttered the strangest words:

> Blessed are you among women, and blessed is the fruit of your womb. And why has this happened to me, that the mother of my Lord comes to me? For as soon as I heard the sound of your greeting, the child in my womb leapt for joy. And blessed is she who believed that there would be a fulfillment of what was spoken to her by the Lord. (Luke 1:42–45)

I was so confused, but Elizabeth told me she was certain my child was to be a special one, just as hers would be. If Elizabeth—whom I had always thought to be the closest person to God I had ever known—if she thought this was a blessing, then maybe my spirit would come to rejoice in this mysterious act, an act that must be of God. But how would I tell Joseph?

When Joseph returned home, he added to my surprise by telling me that he, too, had a dream about this child. He even dreamed the same name: Jesus. Could it be true? Joseph pledged to make me his wife immediately, and it was done.

Near the time for my baby to come, we learned we had to make a trip to Bethlehem for the census. It was decreed by Emperor Augustus, so we had to go. No sooner had we entered the city than the pains began, and I knew the baby was coming. We had to take shelter in a cave that was home to animals because the town was full of visitors for the census.

Joseph went to find a midwife, but this baby of mine would not wait. I was all alone, but I did not feel alone. And even though it was the dark of night, a bright light shone into the mouth of the cave—a bright star illuminating the dark night, shining on the face of my son. Other stars twinkled above, and the sounds of the night sounded like a choir of angels, singing my baby boy to sleep.

Maybe it was from the Evil One, or maybe from my unbelief, but I have thought these many years that I needed to protect my son, but from what? I don't know. From evil? From evil people? From God? From himself? I remember the day we went to the temple to present our newborn boy—after my forty days of purification—with our gifts of two young pigeons. We were just one more poor family, coming to present our child, but people seemed to take special notice of us.

I remember old Anna. She reminded me of my saintly mother who bore the same name and the same spirit. The people who worshipped at the temple and saw her day after day called her a prophet. She touched our son's forehead and praised God for him. She told everyone he would be the redemption of Jerusalem (Luke 2:36–38). What could she mean?

And Simeon, who, I'm told, often said that "he would not see death before he had seen the Lord's Messiah" (Luke 2:26) took our son from my arms into his and said, "Master, now you are dismissing your servant in peace, according to your word; for my eyes have seen your salvation" (Luke 2:29–30). Redemption. Salvation. These strange words from strangers made me even more protective of my son. He belonged to me, not to them!

After our son's birth, we heard something frightening about the king whom the Romans called Herod the Great. He's been anything but great to us Jews. I heard this "great king" feared anyone who might overthrow his kingship, and Joseph told me of an odd dream he had, that Herod was coming for our son. Our son? A baby? Why was the Great King Herod so afraid of a baby that he would order the murder of all the male babies born around Bethlehem, just like the evil Pharaoh did at the time of Moses's birth? Even so, I convinced him to take us to Egypt where we lived for many years before returning to Nazareth after the death of King Herod. How could we know that his son, the next King Herod, would be just as dangerous?

After several years, we were back in Nazareth among friends and family. Wouldn't we be safe there? Even as a child, Jesus loved going to the synagogue in Nazareth, and he never minded the long trek to Jerusalem for the festivals. Such words of wisdom the elders had never heard coming from the mouth of a child, and even the priests were amazed by him (Luke 2:41–50).

I tried to keep him away from the priests, fearing they would want him to serve them. I remembered stories of our ancestor Samuel, how he served the priests at the tabernacle, and I wondered how his mother, Hannah, could bear giving him up when he was but a young boy. But then I remembered my own mother—long past childbearing years—who considered my birth such a miracle that she dedicated me to the temple to serve the priests and God, until dear Joseph took me into his home.

My little Jesus was fascinated by the temple and the priests' conversations, even disobeying me and staying with them when he knew it was time to return home. Once when he was a boy of about twelve, after returning from one of our trips to Jerusalem, he said something that frightened me. He said, "Mother, if you knew that you must die in order to save the world, would you?" What makes a child ask such things? I was afraid to answer the question, afraid even more to hear his answer.

As he grew older, I was desperate to find a way to distract him from what seemed to be a mission—a calling—something he could not escape. I encouraged Joseph to take him on as an apprentice, and I even encouraged them to accept work far away in the king's newest construction project. And then Joseph died, and Jesus returned home to bury his father and mourn with his mother. He was a man now, and it was time for him to find a wife.

But he didn't stay long. He traveled south to the community of Qumran, near the Dead Sea, where a sect of Jews known as Essenes have lived for about two centuries. At first, I was glad he was there—away from Nazareth, away from Jerusalem. But then I learned about the community at Qumran. They commit to celibacy and to preserving the Hebrew scriptures, meticulously copying old worn papyrus scrolls to new ones, and I learned they talk about ideas such as Son of God, Son of Man, Messiah, suffering. When I heard those words, I remembered my dream from so many years ago. I shuddered at the memory.

After many years, Jesus returned to Galilee, and I knew he was a changed man. I followed him from town to town and listened to him as he taught the crowds and healed the sick. Healed the sick! I begged him to come home, but he would not. He wasn't even safe there, in our home of Nazareth. His words one Sabbath—borrowed from the prophet Isaiah—angered the people at our synagogue so much that they threatened to kill him.

He told me about his years with the Essenes, about going into the wilderness for forty days and nights, about why he left Qumran to return to "his people." He told me about his baptism with water and what he called the spirit; he was baptized by his cousin John, the child of my cousin Elizabeth. This John, who ate wild locusts and honey, attracted followers and hecklers, and eventually angered the wrong people, King Herod and his wife Herodias. This new Herod was as bad as the last one. He had John killed and his head brought to Herodias on a platter—just as she requested. Would this be the fate of my son, too? I wondered.

Just last week, when I learned he would leave his dear friends in Bethany and return to Jerusalem, I knew the end was near. Like many other Jews, I wanted to go to Jerusalem for the Passover, but I was afraid my son would encounter danger from those who were threatened by his teachings. I hurried to be with him, and as I paused on the Mount of Olives overlooking the city, I saw a large crowd waving palm branches as a parade passed through the gates of the city. I asked some other pilgrims whom they were celebrating, and they said, "The teacher, Jesus, who heals the sick and raises the dead!" My heart sank; my Jesus was entering the holy city, and everyone would know he was there. I had to be there with him, so I hurried on. I have been with him for the last week, never knowing what day would be his last, which embrace would be our last.

At some point, a mother knows who her children are born to be—sometimes even before they know it themselves. This little lamb, who would run to me from his playmates to tell me he loved me; this little lamb, who was so tenderhearted— why must he be slaughtered? Is it for God's glory like the temple sacrifices? Will he save the people like the sacrificial lamb of the Passover? Cannot the angel of death pass over him? They beat him without mercy, and now he hangs from this crooked tree, blood pouring from his wounds. Please, angel of God, appear to me once again. Appeal to the executioners here to take him down so I can tend his wounds. Please.

The darkness covers the hill of Golgotha. No angel comes to my rescue or to comfort me. His friends John and Mary of Magdala urge me to take shelter. How can I leave my son? I will stay to hear his last words, to breathe into my soul his last breath. When they finally remove his body, I will hold him in my arms as I did when he was a child, but this body that I will hold will not be full of promise, full of life, full of love. I will help prepare his body for burial in the cave of another Joseph, one who loves him like a son. I will weep and mourn, but I am his mother, and I know that his death will fulfill his life's purpose, one he understood even as a child, even when I could not, or would not.

What will happen after he dies? Will he go to Sheol to be with his father, Joseph? If so, soon I will join him. But until then, we will remember him. We will remember his birth; we will remember his words and the miracles that were surely of God. Maybe one day we will rejoice that we have known him. And maybe I will be able to pray again the prayer I prayed with Elizabeth, one that I dared not allow to pass my lips after I left her, for fear that it would come true:

> My soul magnifies the Lord, and my spirit rejoices in God my Savior....

His mercy is for those who fear him from generation to generation....
He has brought down the powerful from their thrones and lifted up the lowly;
He has filled the hungry with good things, and sent the rich away empty.
He has helped his servant Israel, in remembrance of his mercy. (Luke 1:47–54)

20
Jairus's Wife

Luke 4—6; 8:40–56

She was only twelve years old. My only child. A precious child, and so full of spirit, but doesn't every mother say that? Even so, she was sickly from the time she was a baby. We tried everything—for twelve years. The physicians didn't know what to do for her, even the physician Luke who was able to help children like ours get better.

It was only days ago, right before the Sabbath, that I noticed she was particularly weak. She insisted on walking with me to the market, to buy food to prepare our Sabbath meal, but as we returned, she said she needed to stop and rest. By the time we arrived at our home, she was having trouble breathing. I put her to bed and tried all the things the physicians told us to do. But nothing helped.

My mother and cousins came and helped me care for my sick child. The next day was the Sabbath, and though he didn't want to leave us, my husband, Jairus, went to the synagogue at my urging. I reminded him to ask the people to pray for our sick daughter. You see, my husband is a leader of the synagogue—a man of faith.

But while he was gone, our little one became even weaker, gasping for breath. I sent one of our neighbors to the synagogue to bring Jairus home right away. When he arrived, he needed only to glance at our little one to see how ill she was. We crossed to the other side of the room so she would not hear what we had to say.

"Jairus, we must do something," I said. "We must get help." Jairus offered to call for a doctor, but the doctors had already told us there was nothing more they could do. "What about Jesus?" I asked. My husband, usually so strong and confident, looked troubled. He hung his head and said, "We just can't do that. I am a leader of the synagogue. We just can't do that."

We had had that conversation many times before. You see, I had heard about Jesus, who was from the family of Joseph in Nazareth. I heard of him from some friends, and I was determined to meet him. He had been traveling around Galilee teaching in synagogues, and many who heard him were amazed at the power and authority with which he spoke. Some called him rabbi; some called him Messiah. But others, including many at our synagogue, called him blasphemer.

Who was this man? They said even the demons obeyed him! I talked to people who saw him heal a man's withered hand in the synagogue one day, and do you know what the leaders did? They criticized him for violating the laws of the Sabbath. Some of my friends who followed him said they saw people cured from leprosy, fevers, even paralysis. I was determined to see him for myself.

One day my mother and I followed the crowds to a place where we heard he would be. I didn't tell my husband I was going; he would not have approved. We came to a plain where hundreds, maybe thousands, were gathered, waiting to hear him. The people pressed close to Jesus, but his followers tried to keep them at a distance. They all wanted to touch him. I wanted to touch him too, but I was too far away, so I could only listen to him. I was drawn to him—even from a distance.

I've tried, but I cannot find words to describe Jesus to you: gentle but strong, with a voice that stilled the rumblings of the crowd. He spoke words that brought tears to the eyes of grown men and women, words that confused even the learned ones. Unlike many of our great teachers and leaders, he didn't speak arrogantly of himself. He spoke to us. He challenged us. He helped us to understand God. Listen to some of the things he said:

> Love your enemies, do good to those who hate you, bless those who curse you, pray for those who abuse you. If anyone strikes you on the cheek, offer the other also; and from anyone who takes away your coat, do not withhold even your shirt. Give to everyone who begs from you; and if anyone takes away your goods, do not ask for them again. Do to others as you would have them do to you. (Luke 6:27–31)

His words were difficult to understand—but they held such truth. He said:

> If you love those who love you, what credit is that to you? For even sinners love those who love them. If you do good to those who do good to you, what credit is that to you? For even the sinners do the same. If you lend to those from whom you hope to receive, what credit is that to you? Even sinners lend to sinners, to receive as much again. But love your enemies, do good, and lend, expecting nothing in return. Your reward will be great, and you will be children of the Most High; for he is kind to the ungrateful and the wicked. Be merciful, just as your Father is merciful. (Luke 6:32–36)

Then he said:

> Do not judge, and you will not be judged; do not condemn, and you will not be condemned. Forgive, and you will be forgiven; give, and it will be given to you. (Luke 6:37–38)

His words burned into my very soul. I said them over and over when I left that day. As I hurried home to prepare our evening meal, I wondered if I could ever love the way he taught that we should love. What would it mean to love my enemies? Love the Samaritans? Love the Romans? How? And what would it mean to give in the way he taught us that we should give? My family is wealthy, and I have come to enjoy our wealth. But he said to give. Give and forgive.

That night, I told my husband about hearing Jesus. I told him every word I could remember. I told him how my heart changed that day. And I told him of an overwhelming feeling of love, that I was, indeed, loved by God, and that I could love others as God loved me. I thought he would be angry, but he was not. I think he was afraid. Afraid that he would lose the respect of other leaders of the synagogue. Afraid that he would lose business if people found out his wife was one of those who followed Jesus of Nazareth. Afraid that people would be cruel to me.

That was the look that I saw in his face as we wondered what we could do to help our daughter. It was the look of fear. "Jairus," I begged, "if you are afraid to go yourself, I will go. Just look at her! She will soon die. Please, my love. Go find Jesus." At that moment, I must have had enough faith for both of us, and he agreed. "I will go," he said. "I will go because I believe in you, and you believe in Jesus." And so, he left.

Have you ever known a time when your own faith was as weak as a strand of thread, but you knew you must be strong for others around you? I returned to our daughter's bedside and took her tiny, frail body into my arms, sitting up with her to ease her breathing. I sang her favorite songs from childhood. "Please, God," I prayed, "help my husband find Jesus very soon—before it's too late."

I sang and prayed and rocked my child until we both slept. I awoke moments later, aware that the little body in my arms felt different. She was so limp. I spoke to her, but she didn't answer. "Oh please, God, not my daughter—*my only child*. She is only twelve years old." But she was gone. It was too late for Jesus.

I sent a cousin to find my husband and tell him not to trouble Jesus any longer. My mother and cousins helped me prepare my daughter's body for burial, and we wailed with grief as we tended to her. Through our wailing, I thought I heard someone shout, "They're coming, and Jesus is with them!" But it was too late for Jesus.

My husband entered the house with Jesus and his friends Peter, James, and John. Jesus asked my mother and cousins and everyone else to leave the room. All that remained were Jesus, Peter, James, John, my husband, and me. Jesus walked over to our little one and "took her by the hand and called out, 'Child, get up!'" (Luke 8:54). And she did.

I do not understand miracles, but I have just witnessed one. I do not understand faith, but I have it. I do not understand Jesus, but I believe in him. And though I have tried, I cannot explain any of it, but my daughter can. I asked her last night, as I helped her climb into bed, "What did Jesus do to make you well?" Her eyes grew wide, and with the faith of a child, she said, "Oh mother, he just touched me, and the moment his hand touched mine, I felt strong again."

He touched me too, not my hand but my soul. This Jesus who would dare to touch a corpse. This Jesus who would dare to touch a leper. This Jesus who would dare to touch a tax collector and a sinner, this Jesus touched me. I will never be the same again. And you? If I tell you where you can find Jesus, will you go find him? He will touch you, too. I know he will.

21
The Samaritan Woman

John 4:1–42
With Reference to the Story of Tamar (Genesis 38)

Have you ever felt despised? Hated because of your heritage, or your faith, or the color of your skin? Have you ever mistreated or despised another because of her race or his family of origin? Come into my world. You see, I am a Samaritan and a woman.

I live in Sychar, a town near the ancient city of Shechem. Our town is in the land known as Samaria, between Judea and Galilee. Once we were part of the great nation of Israel—the land promised to our fathers: Abraham, Isaac, Jacob, and Joseph. We started as twelve tribes, related by blood, but divided by land, by greed, by politics.

And then about one thousand years ago we became a united kingdom under our great King David, but when King David's son Solomon died about nine hundred years ago, the kingdom divided once again, with ten northern tribes aligning as Israel, part of which is now known as Samaria, and two southern tribes forming Judah, now known as Judea. I often wonder why our ancestors allowed those ancient animosities, even within our large family, to divide us. Why do we continue that sin—even today?

You see, we all worshiped the same God, Yahweh, but soon we northerners were not welcomed in the house of the Lord, the great temple in Jerusalem. In time, we built our own place of worship—ours at Mt. Gerizim—and like our brothers and sisters in Jerusalem, we, too, were unfaithful to Yahweh and welcomed the gods and goddesses of the Canaanites, and later the Greeks, into our worship. We both did, but to hear the Jews of Judea and Galilee talk, you'd think we were the only ones with leaders like Ahab and Jezebel who worshipped Baal and his consort, Asherah.

And then came the Assyrians. About seven hundred years ago, they came from the north and conquered our great nation of Israel. They forced our people to marry with them. This was especially true for the women, who are always vulnerable to the conquerors. And they forced us to worship their gods. For this, the Jews call us dogs.

I am trapped between two worlds: Canaanite and Jewish. You see, my family has remained faithful to Yahweh. We observe the Laws of Moses, and we honor the Torah. Like women of Judea, I am bound by the same laws that offer blessings and curses to women. One of those laws says if a woman's husband dies before she gives birth to his son, she must be given to his brother to be his brother's wife—to give sons to the deceased brother. I know it sounds confusing, but it is the "law of brothers"—the *levirate* law. This was the case with our ancestor Tamar.

Have you heard her story? Tamar was given first to the son of Judah, Er, who died. She was then given to his brother Onan, who also died, and when Judah refused to give her to his third son, Shelah, Tamar disguised herself as a prostitute when Judah came to shear his sheep and became pregnant by her father-in-law. Isn't it ironic: he would take a prostitute—which was against the Law—but he would not obey the levirate law. You can find this story in our Book of Genesis in the Torah. Tamar became the mother of Perez and Zerah, sons AND grandsons of Judah—twins whose battle in their mother's womb to see who would be born first reminds me of how the people of Israel have battled for God's favor.

I think of Tamar often, for my life is much like hers. I have been given to five brothers, and each one has died from a similar illness that travels through this family. Some have called me a witch.

No man wants to marry me now, and the one who protects me has another wife. But unlike Tamar, I have no sons to comfort me. The women shun me when I come to the well of Jacob to draw water, whether in the cool of the morning or evening. That is why I often come in the heat of the noonday sun. I will do anything to avoid the harsh glances of my neighbors.

Neighbor. What is a neighbor? I confess that I am often hurt and disappointed by the treatment I receive from my neighbors, but I cannot say I expect more from those who travel through Samaria.

Let me explain. Jews traveling between Judea and Galilee travel through Samaria to take the shortest route, and though they despise all of us, they must stop for water or food or lodging. That is another reason why the other women go to the well early or late in the day, to avoid the foreign travelers. But in my hope to avoid the women, I often meet these travelers when they seek water at the well of our ancestors. They are cruel, shouting to me, "Fetch me water, you dog, and keep your unclean hands off the rim of the jar." You see, Jews believe that all Samaritans are unclean. I've even heard them say that Samaritan women bleed from birth, making us ritually unclean—perpetually unclean.

That's why I was so surprised several days ago when a Jew stopped for water on his way from Judea to Galilee. It was about noon, and I was at the well of Jacob. It was hot and dusty that day; no breeze fanned the trees, and the sun scorched my face as I drew the heavy bucket out of the deep well. He looked so tired as he parted ways with his fellow travelers. What long journey has made his body weary, I wondered?

As they parted, I could tell by their gestures that they respected him...cared for him...loved him. They called him "Rabbi," and I heard them say they were going into town for food. He looked sad. Perhaps, I thought, he, too, knew what it meant to be despised. I turned back to my work, hurriedly completing my task so I could depart from what would, surely, be another hurtful—perhaps even dangerous—encounter with a man.

And then, he approached me. He kindly asked for a drink. A Jew, but not just a Jew; he was a rabbi, speaking to a woman who was alone. Unheard of.

"How is it that you, a Jew, ask a drink of me, a woman of Samaria," I asked (John 4:9).

Even before he answered, I saw in his face a look of such kindness, of wisdom, like looking into the face of an angel—though I confess I've never seen an angel. And then he spoke to me, "If you knew the gift of God, and who it is that is saying to you, 'give me a drink,' you would have asked him, and he would have given you living water" (John 4:10).

I knew he was speaking figuratively, but I had never had such a conversation with a man. I continued, "Sir, you have no bucket and the well is deep. Where do you get that living water? Are you greater than our ancestor Jacob, who gave us the well, and with his sons and his flocks, drank from it?" (John 4:11). His response confused me. He said:

> Everyone who drinks of this water will be thirsty again, but those who drink of the water that I will give them will never be thirsty. The water that I will give will become in them a spring of water gushing up to eternal life. (John 4:13–14)

Eternal life. I often think about what happens after we die. Our Hebrew tradition tells us that blessings and curses manifest themselves in our lifetimes, and that with death we simply go to the abode of the dead: Sheol. But there are some among us who believe that our spirits live on after death.

"Sir," I said, my voice trembling with uncertainty, "give me this water, so that I may never be thirsty or have to keep coming here to draw water" (John 4:15). I must have said something wrong, because just then the conversation changed, and I wondered if he would be like all the others. "Go call your husband and come back," he said (John 4:16). "I have no husband," I replied in all honesty (John 4:17). His reply stunned me. Could he see into my mind? See into my soul? He responded, "You are right in saying, I have no husband, for you have had five husbands, and the one you have now is not your husband. What you have said is true!" (John 4:18)

Surely, he is nothing like the others, I thought. If he is a man of God, I will ask him to help me understand things that I often talk to God about, things that I often wonder about. "Sir, I see that you are a prophet. Our ancestors worshipped on this mountain, but you say that the place where people must worship is in Jerusalem" (John 4:19–20). And he responded:

> Woman, believe me, the hour is coming when you will worship the Father neither on this mountain nor in Jerusalem. You worship what you do not know; we worship what we know, [that] salvation is from the Jews. But the hour is coming, and is now here, when the true worshippers will worship the Father in spirit and truth, for the Father seeks such as these to worship him. God is spirit, and those who worship him must worship in spirit and truth. (John 4:21–24)

Could it be? Could he be the one? I almost shouted, "I know that Messiah is coming (who is called Christ). When he comes, he will proclaim all things to us" (John 4:25). And then he confirmed what I believed—in the deepest part of me—with these words: "I am he, the one who is speaking to you" (John 4:26).

I gasped. At that very moment, I had so many questions, but our conversation was suddenly interrupted when his friends returned. I could tell they were shocked to find him speaking to me, a Samaritan and a woman. I left my jugs of water and hurried off, running back to the city of Sychar as quickly as I could. I couldn't wait to tell anyone who would listen about this man who told me everything I had ever done, who spoke of living water and eternal life, who spoke of God as a loving father. Come, I urged them, come and see him for yourself.

I felt inspired, called by God and his Messiah, Jesus! I was able to convince many people to come and listen to Jesus, and they, too, became believers. Jesus stayed with us for two days, not long enough, but in that time, our lives were changed by his teaching.

When he left, many said, "We know that this is truly the Savior of the world" (John 4:42).

How odd. I am not allowed to count toward quorum for synagogue, and my testimony is not valid for legal matters. Most Jewish men would dare not speak to me or drink water from my cup. But this prophet of God trusted me to carry his words to my people. I long to hear more about his ministry, as he travels first to Galilee and then back to Jerusalem. He has enemies, I'm told, but a group of women follow him and provide for him. I will pray to God that they will protect him. I will pray to God that they will comfort him. I will pray to God that men and women and children who need to know the love of God will hear him, and will say, as many do today in Sychar: "We know that this man really is the Savior of the world" (adapted from John 4:42).

22
The Woman Caught in Adultery

John 8:1–11

Note: Luke 8:2–3 introduces us to Joanna—wife of Herod's steward, Chuza—who was among the "women who had been cured of evil spirits and infirmities" and followed Jesus. While there is no biblical evidence that Chuza was associated with the woman caught in adultery in the Gospel of John, this story imagines how the wife of Herod's steward might have become an independent and grateful woman who followed Jesus. Biblical background on Herod Antipas comes from Mark's and Matthew's Gospels and biblical history.

At first, I was honored by his lustful looks. After all, he was a steward in Herod's court. His name was Chuza, and he managed the household affairs of the tetrarch of Galilee and Perea, Herod Antipas. You may have heard of Herod's father, King Herod the Great. I never knew why they called him great. I heard he feared any threat to his power. About thirty years ago, he even had all the baby boys in his kingdom killed when he heard the fortune tellers say that a baby had been born who would become king. And then he had his own son killed for fear his son would overthrow him.

This Herod—Antipas, another son—is anything but great, but he loves to be called King. Chuza told me he divorced his wife and took as another wife Herodias—his niece and sister-in-law—wife of his brother Philip (Mark 6). You can imagine the stir caused by that marriage. His first wife's father, King Aretas IV of Nabatea, was furious, and arguments between the families resulted in the division of King Herod's territory into four regions upon his death. This Herod, Antipas, got the weakest region—Galilee—the region where my family has lived for generations.

I saw Chuza often at the market where I worked. He would oversee purchases for Herod's household, and while his servants filled his baskets, he would come to my shop and find a reason to take me behind the curtain. I knew it was wrong, and I knew it was against the laws of our ancestor Moses, but I didn't mind. He brought me gifts and gave me a coin or two each time. He was kind and gentle, not mean and rough like many men. And I felt sorry for him. He told me his wife, Joanna, was filled with an evil spirit and didn't love him like I did.

I'd heard that before. That's what most men say when they try to convince other women to meet their needs. But still, I felt sorry for him, especially when he told me she took his money and left him. Left him to follow the latest so-called Messiah, one named Jesus of Nazareth. I hear she travels with Jesus and his disciples, along with some other women. How shameful! But who am I to talk about shame?

One day Chuza told me a story so horrific that I did not believe him. He said he had planned a special celebration for Herod's birthday, and for entertainment, he arranged for Herodias's daughter, Salome, to dance for her stepfather. Herod had consumed many glasses of the best wine, and after her dance, he told her to name a prize for her dance. She leaned in to her mother and asked, "What shall I request, Mother?" And her mother whispered, "Ask for the head of John the Baptist—on a platter." (See Matt 14:1–12 and Mark 6:14–29; the historian Josephus names the daughter Salome.)

I had heard of this man known as John the Baptist. He preached and baptized people in the Jordan River, dressed only in a loincloth of animal skin. I heard he only ate wild locusts and honey (Mark 1:4–6). None of that would have drawn the attention of Herod, had he not criticized the tetrarch for his marriage and accused him of adultery. That landed him in jail, and only moments after Salome uttered her request to her king, some men arrived with the Baptist's head in a sack. The chore fell to Chuza to arrange it on a platter and deliver it to the king. He said it was the most sickening chore he ever fulfilled for his ruler. He was still trembling with fear and disgust when he came to see me the following day.

But he came with an interesting proposal: "Come with me to Jerusalem," he said. "I must go on an errand for my Lord, Herod, and we can spend many days together where no one will know us." I knew what he meant. It's the Feast of Booths for the Jews, and there would be many people there. I was happy to go to the City of David, happy to see the grand temple, happy to escape the boredom of Galilee. We made the journey to Jerusalem, and there we were able to enjoy each other's company during the day without hiding and enjoy each other in comfort during nights at the local inn.

One day we went to the temple where we heard the local people complaining about a visitor from Galilee, Jesus of Nazareth, who was drawing the ire of the religious leaders. I heard the temple police talking to the chief priests who asked them, "Why did you not arrest him?" The police answered, "Never has anyone spoken like this!" (John 7:45–46). I'd heard of this Jesus—from people in Galilee. I'd heard of him from Chuza. He was the prophet for whom Joanna, wife of Chuza, left her husband!

The next day when we returned to the temple, I had a feeling of foreboding danger—not knowing why—and then out of the corner of one eye I spotted some women whom I recognized from Galilee. One was Mary of Magdala and the other was Joanna, Chuza's wife! I tried to steer him away from the group of women, but it was too late. One of the women shouted, "There is Chuza, steward of Herod, husband of Joanna—with another woman!" I was frozen, as stiff as the Roman statues that honor their Caesars, and suddenly I was surrounded by some men who grabbed me by the arm. They were the temple police, and they accused me of adultery.

Adultery. Our law says, "You shall not commit adultery" (Exod 20:14) and "If a man commits adultery with the wife of his neighbor, both the adulterer and the adulteress shall be put to death" (Lev 20:10). I have known women who were literally caught in the act of adultery with men—and both were found guilty and executed. But more often I have known unmarried women who became pregnant, and only they were accused and executed. I've also known unmarried women who accused men of raping them, but since there were no witnesses—or perhaps the alleged rape occurred out in the countryside where nobody could have heard her call for help—the accusation of rape was seen as a confession of adultery.

I have always wondered if Moses was only talking to the men when he said, "You shall not commit adultery," because I've always been told that adultery is a property law, and women cannot hold property. We can *be* property, though, and if one man takes another man's property—his woman—that is adultery.

And now I have been accused.

While the temple police were arguing among themselves, I saw Chuza nervously hand one of them a purse filled with coins, and then he slipped quietly away. Why did I not suspect that he would save himself rather than me? One of the scribes came over to see what the commotion was, and I heard him whisper to the police, "This is our chance to trap the rabbi with his own laws. Let's go find him." As I looked around for Chuza, they grabbed me and began to drag me away. I screamed for Chuza, but he never came to my rescue.

After that everything was a blur. By the time we got to the place where Jesus was teaching some of his followers, the police had gathered a crowd of more scribes and Pharisees. Along the way they taunted me and shoved me back and forth among them. I was shaken, my long hair loose, my shawl left somewhere along the way, my dress torn, my face streaked with tears.

And then they saw Jesus, seated near the temple, with people gathered around, listening to his teachings. They made me stand before Jesus and they said, "Teacher, this woman was caught in the very act of committing adultery. Now in the law Moses commanded us to stone such women. Now what do you say?" (John 8:5). I knew they were just testing him. I heard them outline their plot along the way. Jesus came close to me and wrote in the sand. He didn't look at me, but I looked at the message as it was written: "Where is the man?" I'm sure my accusers saw the message too, and they knew the law, but they didn't answer the question. They just "kept on questioning him" (John 8:7).

All around us, men were shouting insults at me and questions at Jesus, but it was as if he heard nothing. "He straightened up and said to them, 'Let anyone among you who is without sin be the first to throw a stone at her.' And once again he bent down and wrote on the ground" (John 8:7–8).

I read his second message, and then I followed his eyes as he looked up and stared into the crowd. Only then did I see Chuza, standing in the front of the crowd. Chuza looked down and read the words: "Which one among you is the man?" He quickly turned around and left, followed by the man with the purse of coins, and then another and another until I was left alone with Jesus. Again, he straightened up and said, "Woman, where are they? Has no one condemned you?" (John 8:10). I replied, "No one, sir." And Jesus said, "Neither do I condemn you. Go your way, and from now on do not sin again" (John 8:11).

To be honest, I never thought that what I was doing with Chuza was sinful. Yes, he was violating his marriage vows, and yes, I was being dishonest to go willingly to this man. But in the eyes of the law, I was a sinner, an adulteress, and worthy of death. Why not him? Why are the laws of adultery levied against women more than men? Why is it legal for a man to rape a woman if she is not married or betrothed to be married? The law says he must marry her, so one might argue that is his punishment and her protection, but she was a virgin! Why is that not punishable by our laws?

You may wonder what happened to me. I left Jerusalem to return to Galilee and resume my life. I never spoke to Chuza again. I hear he returned to his job with Herod Antipas and his life with Joanna. I heard she was miraculously healed of her evil spirit. The women of Galilee shun me. The men of Galilee shun me. I am tainted. I am an adulteress, even though I have not known another man since Chuza. But when my solitary existence becomes too much to bear, I remember that day in the City of David when one man saved my life and saw me as a person, not a sinner, and I will be forever grateful to the man named Jesus.

23
Mary Magdalene

Based Primarily on the Gospel of Luke

I used to be possessed—possessed by demons. One day I would feel like I was crawling out of my skin, and the next day I would cry for hours without even knowing why I was sad. Then I would become filled with anger, and I would shout hateful things to everyone around me. I never knew what would happen next. It seemed as if a different demon possessed me each day of the week. "She's the woman with seven demons," they would say, and then they'd spit on me or throw stones at me, or just ignore me.

My name is Mary. I live in the town of Magdala, on the western edge of the Sea of Galilee. Well, I should say I *lived* there. I haven't been welcome in my hometown for years. Even though I have changed, they will not accept me. But Jesus did.

Have you met Jesus? Before I met him, I had no hope. No hope for friends or family, no hope for a husband, no hope for the future. Fortunately, I was blessed—or cursed, I don't know which—with a gift for making exquisite pottery. When I was well, I could work for hours without stopping...or even sleeping. But days of almost euphoric activity would give way to days of deep despair. I didn't want to see anyone, and I didn't want to leave my home; all I wanted to do was sit in the dark...alone...or sleep for hours on end. What misery!

Oh, but I made large sums of money selling my pottery to strangers who came through Magdala. The strangers weren't afraid of me; how could they know? I had plenty of money. In a way, that was a curse too. The townspeople all knew I was a gifted potter, but they talked about my money behind my back, saying, "Mary of Magdala, how is she so wealthy? Does she entertain men in her home? Sometimes we don't see her for days, and her windows are closed. How much do her visitors pay for...entertainment?"

Finally, I decided to leave Magdala and move north to Capernaum, a larger town on the shore of the Sea of Galilee. Perhaps, I thought, I could leave my troubles behind me. Perhaps I could start over. Perhaps the people in Capernaum wouldn't notice my demons. Maybe, just maybe, the demons would stay in Magdala.

No sooner had I arrived and settled in Capernaum than I heard that someone else was new in the town. His name was Jesus, and he was from Nazareth. He was a gifted teacher, and he had special powers from God. He could heal the sick, cause the lame to walk, raise people from the dead, and even command demons to go away. People would crowd around him wherever he went screaming, "Touch me, Jesus. Bless me, Jesus. Heal me, Jesus." He didn't care who touched him: old, young, rich, poor, unclean, tax collectors, women. He would eat with people that most rabbis would never even visit. I could tell you stories about what I saw him do, but you probably would not believe me.

I first heard him teach one Sabbath in the synagogue. He was different. He spoke with authority and power, but sometimes he spoke in parables that were difficult to understand. He challenged us to rethink what we believed, what it means to be God's people, and what it means to observe God's laws—even laws about the Sabbath. He would say things like, "If you love those who love you, what credit is that to you? For even sinners love those who love them" (Luke 6:32).

I could see the men in the synagogue whispering to each other when he spoke. Many of them were furious. I heard some of our most important leaders among the Pharisees say vicious, threatening things about him, and I feared for his safety. I understand he was driven out of the synagogue in his hometown of Nazareth. Perhaps he knew how it feels to be hopeless, to be scorned, to be cast out by friends and family.

But you would never know it to hear him; he never seemed afraid. He was not concerned about himself, but he was concerned about us. He spoke to us with such compassion. He would always bless us—the poor, the hungry, those who weep, those who are hated and excluded and reviled. And then he would say to us, "Bless those who curse you, and pray for those who abuse you" (Luke 6:28). He would encourage us, especially when we were criticized for our beliefs. He would say, "Rejoice in that day and leap for joy, for surely your reward is great in heaven" (Luke 6:23). He talked about the kingdom of heaven often. I never quite understood what he meant by that. At times, he talked about it as if it were a place. More often, he spoke of it as being one with God. Sometimes he talked about it as something to look forward to in the future, but more often he implied that it was available to us right now. His words were powerful, but his actions were even more powerful. I know.

One day I followed the crowds from the synagogue to the seashore to hear him. Then, after hours of teaching us, he slipped away from the crowds to rest. I walked over to where he was resting, and he seemed to be deep in prayer. "Rabbi," I said, as I approached him, "may I talk to you?" He invited me to sit with him, and he listened as I told him my story. I told him the part about the demons, the part about the anger, the part about the suspicions of my neighbors and family—the whole story.

I told him I felt like such a sinner, so unworthy of God's love. I dared not look at him, partly because my head was hung in shame, and partly because I knew how inappropriate it was that I, a woman, would speak to a man in public—especially one we called "Rabbi." And then he gently took my face in his hands. He lifted my face and looked into my eyes. I cannot describe the power that I felt run through my body as he looked at me. And he said, "Woman, your sins are forgiven. And as for your demons, they are no more. Go in peace."

What did he mean? My demons are no more? In the days that followed, I still laughed out loud and cried for no reason, and I confess that I still get angry at times. But I have felt like a new person ever since that day he looked—not only into my eyes, but into my very soul. I finally realized what he meant. My demons are no more. No longer must they control my life. Not anymore. He healed my *spirit.*

What can one do when someone promises hope where there seemed to be none? What can one do when someone promises a way where there seems to be no way? What can one do when someone takes away the fear of death and offers the promise of new life? What would you do? What could I do? Only one thing. Give him my life. And I did. In fact, I gave him all the money I had saved to support his ministry, and I volunteered to travel with him and his inner circle of twelve disciples.

He called us all his disciples. He welcomed me as one of them, along with Joanna; Susanna; Mary, wife of Clopas; Salome; and Mary of Bethany and her sister, Martha. There were so many. Oh, but the men didn't necessarily agree with Jesus about including the women; in fact, I heard them say to one another, "Doesn't our tradition say, 'Better the Torah be burned than to fall into the hands of a woman?'" But they wouldn't dare question his decision.

We women sat at his feet along with the Twelve. We discussed the scriptures and learned from him. That is something that women in my culture simply do not do. He sent us out in pairs to proclaim the kingdom of God and to heal the sick, but he told us it would not be easy. It wasn't, but what we were able to accomplish in the name of God was nothing short of miraculous. When we returned to him, he looked at us with such understanding, knowing what we had endured, and said, "Blessed are the eyes that see what you see" (Luke 10:23).

Maybe I don't have those eyes yet, because I don't understand what has happened in the last few weeks. We decided to go to Jerusalem for the Passover celebration, even though many of Jesus's followers thought it would be too dangerous. His reputation preceded him, you see, and the religious and political leaders in Jerusalem had heard stories about how popular he was in Galilee. Perhaps you have heard about what happened next. He was arrested while praying in a garden, right after we celebrated the Feast of Unleavened Bread. Jesus was questioned by the Sanhedrin, by Pilate, and by Herod, and he was eventually sentenced to die by crucifixion. The day he died was one of the darkest days of my life. I had not known such despair since before Jesus cast the demons out of me.

I saw him breathe his last breath. Joanna was there with me, along with Mary, the mother of James, and some of the other women who traveled with us. I don't know where the other disciples were... scared, perhaps, that they would be arrested next. The Sabbath was about to begin—at sundown—so we had to go home right after they laid him in the tomb. We couldn't even prepare his body with burial spices. We had to wait until Sunday morning. We stayed together through the Sabbath, devastated, trying to make sense of everything. But nothing made sense.

And then on Sunday morning, we went to the tomb and saw that it was empty. Suddenly, out of nowhere, two men with garments as bright as the stars said to us, "Why do you look for the living among the dead? He is not here, but has risen" (Luke 24:5). And then we remembered that he had told us—back in Galilee—that this would happen! We ran to tell the disciples, but they didn't believe us! Peter was the only one who would return to the tomb with us, and he saw that it was empty. And then, little by little, they began to believe. Some of us have felt his presence with us just as if he were still here...felt the breeze as if he was breathing on us his favorite words: "Peace be with you" (John 20:19).

And some—including me—insist, no matter how absurd it may sound, that we have seen him. We know we will be reunited with him in God's heavenly kingdom, and we know that he lives in our hearts every day.

Have you met Jesus? If you haven't, I hope you will, and very soon. He will change your life, too, just as he has changed mine.

24
Phoebe

Romans 16:1–2; Excerpts from Romans, 1 Corinthians, Galatians

Greetings! My name is Phoebe, and I am a resident of Cenchreae in the southern part of Achaia. I believe you call it Greece. My town is a port on the eastern side of the Peloponnesian peninsula, about eight thousand paces from Corinth, as the Romans measure distance. You would call that eight miles. Not far.

We are an important port city because the ships come here from the east—from Ephesus and Jerusalem—either to unload their goods for the trek across land to Corinth for shipping to Rome and the west, or to pull the ships onto land and convey them across by human and animal power to avoid the treacherous open waters. Can you imagine the effort needed to avoid sailing around the coast to the Great Sea? I heard the emperor declare he would dig a canal to connect the two seas one day. A canal as deep as the ocean? Never!

You may be surprised to hear a woman talk of politics and shipping routes, but I am proud of my role in Cenchreae's economy. Since the untimely death of my husband, I have managed our business alone—and very successfully!

As you can see from my jewelry and fine clothing, I am a wealthy woman, but I have begun to use my wealth in new ways since I met a wonderful man named Paul of Tarsus and learned from him about

Jesus, who we call Messiah. I have provided funds for Paul's growing ministry, including funds to establish a congregation of Christians in Cenchreae. You see, I believe God has given me many material blessings, not to use for my benefit but to use to glorify God, and I am honored to return to God a portion of those blessings. I am also honored to use my gifts of leadership to glorify God, to minister to the congregation at Cenchreae through the office of deacon.

Let me tell you about my friends in Cenchreae. We are called "Christians" because we believe that Jesus of Nazareth is the Messiah, the Christ of God. It has been two decades since the death and resurrection of Jesus, and the only account we have of the life of Jesus is what we know from Paul and some others from Jerusalem who knew Jesus. I hope one day we will have a written record about Jesus and all of his miraculous deeds, but for now, we will simply have to listen to the stories.

I should tell you how I met Paul. I first saw him standing in the market in Corinth. His looks were not remarkable, but his voice and his message were. He debated with the philosophers in the marketplace—men from Corinth, Athens, and Sparta—and he invited all people, those in high standing as well as laborers and slaves, to hear the good news of our Lord Jesus Christ. He debated, too, with the Jews in the synagogue. I heard him say many times, "There is no longer Jew or Greek, there is no longer slave or free, there is no longer male and female; for all of you are one in Christ Jesus" (Gal 3:28).

I was immediately drawn to this man who preached a compelling message of grace and forgiveness of sins and who encouraged women to join the work and worship of the church along with the men. I understand Jesus did the same, and I have heard stories of women who participated in his ministry, women like Mary of Magdala, Joanna, Susanna, sisters Mary and Martha, and so many others.

I am a Greek woman; I have grown up surrounded by gods and goddesses: Apollo *and Athena*, Poseidon *and Demeter*, Zeus *and Hera*, Aphrodite, Artemis. I come from the ancient tradition of the oracle at Delphi—the priestess to whom men came from miles away to hear prophecy from the gods. Now I worship one God, but I have the same question for all the religions. Why is it that the men think God's power is reserved only for them?

Perhaps that is why I felt so comfortable around Paul—and challenged by his call to faith. He is different from other men, and he offers a different way to understand God through Jesus—to all of us, men and women. You see, there is so much immorality in Corinth and surrounding areas, and there are many divisions—cultural, religious, ethnic, and social. But Paul challenged us to be different, to produce the "fruit of the Spirit" as he calls it, and above all to love.

I do not understand the things I have begun to hear about Paul. Some say he does not value women. How can they say such a thing? I know he holds in highest esteem Priscilla, who, with her husband, Aquila, has a church in their home in Ephesus. Paul met them through their common guild: they are all in the tent-making trade. I met them in Corinth, and they told me that Paul enlisted them to provide counsel to Apollos, an eloquent young man who only preached baptism by John. I also know that Paul enlisted the help of a woman named Lydia to assemble a congregation in Philippi—a congregation that is now thriving. Lydia is a businesswoman like me; I have heard of her work selling purple dyes, and I am pleased that she, too, is using her wealth to spread the gospel.

Paul came to Cenchreae with Priscilla and Aquila before they left for Ephesus, and it was here—in my church—that Paul sealed the vow he made to God by shaving his head. I was honored to participate in that ceremony in my role as a leader of the church at Cenchreae. And now Paul has recruited me to deliver a message he recently wrote to some Christians in Rome. What trust he has shown in me! Along with this letter I am carrying for him, he sent a word of commendation that says:

> I commend to you our sister Phoebe, a deacon of the church at Cenchreae, so that you may welcome her in the Lord as is fitting for the saints, and help her in whatever she may require from you, for she has been a benefactor of many and of myself as well. (Rom 16:1–2)

What kind words; he has no scorn for me—an unmarried woman. And he recognizes the office to which I was consecrated—the office of deacon. I even heard Paul say that women could choose not to be married in order to serve the Lord, but I have also heard him struggle with the Jewish and Greek traditions about women and men.

One of the traditions Paul has struggled with is that of veiling. This issue of veiling is complicated. Some of the Greek women are accustomed to worshipping unveiled, and many of the Jewish women in Corinth are removing their coverings while worshipping as they do at home. I did hear Paul say that women should be veiled, but I tell you, he has only discussed veiling in the context of praying and prophesying in worship (1 Cor 11:2–16). He believes that we should pray and prophesy. I have heard some people say that Paul believes women should not speak in the churches (1 Cor 14:34). How could we pray and prophesy without speaking? Surely someone has started a rumor attributing words to Paul that were not his own. I hope the rumor does not spread.

Many women are involved in the ministry of our growing Christian congregations, serving in various positions of leadership. But there is disagreement about who should lead; in some cases, the disagreements are causing divisions in congregations. I hope your congregations do not suffer from such disagreements. I saw Timothy recently in Corinth, and he told me of some of the current debate about church leadership. One group wants to identify basic moral, ethical, and religious standards for church leaders. They want to ensure that our leaders are people of integrity and of mature faith. But another group wants to define exactly what is meant by integrity and mature faith. Some are saying women should not hold office. Does that mean they do not think women exhibit integrity and mature faith? Excluding women from ministry would be just as devastating—and unjustified—as excluding ministers based on whether they were married. I hope neither ever happens.

Timothy said he knew of some who were even attributing such opinions to Paul. I desperately hope that he is wrong. But I must admit, not everyone in my congregation approved of my consecration to the office of deacon. Some said I had to promise never to marry again. What difference does that make? Others said I could serve the women, but not the men. Others said I could take care of the physical needs of the women and the men, but I could not participate in the baptisms or Holy Eucharist. They say that women defile the altar of the Lord, especially in the times of our impurities.

I pray that these superstitions and restrictions will never become rules in our churches. And I pray that the church of the future will focus on the things of the spirit and not of the flesh.

I think I understand why some people want to restrict women's leadership in the church. You see, we bring to our new Christian congregations many different cultures and beliefs. Some of us were raised in the Greek and Roman traditions, some were earlier converts to Judaism, and we even have a few in our congregation who came from Jerusalem who have never known any faith but faith in Jesus the Christ. And there is so much immorality in our midst. Some say that women should dress modestly—and even keep silent—so that we Christians will be distinguished from the pagans.

And what does Paul say? You see, Paul's words carry such authority, whether he speaks directly or writes letters to us. More than talking about dress and speech and hair, Paul speaks about behavior and actions and faith. He always says to us, "The one who is righteous will live by faith" (Rom 1:17), and "I want you to be wise in what is good and guileless in what is evil" (Rom 16:19). He appeals to us all—the brothers and sisters in the faith—"to present [our] bodies as a living sacrifice, holy and acceptable to God" (Rom 12:1).

And so that is what I will do: present myself to God as a living sacrifice. I thank God that Paul introduced me to the Christian faith and its church, and I thank God that I have been called to the ministry of that blessed church. I pray that you will call women into the ministry of your church, just as I have been called.